# English Grammar for Students of Latin

Norma Goldman

Ladislas Szymanski

*Wayne State University*

The Olivia and Hill Press, Inc.
P.O. Box 7396
Ann Arbor, Michigan 48107

**English Grammar** series
edited by Jacqueline Morton

**English Grammar for Students of French**
**English Grammar for Students of Spanish**
**English Grammar for Students of German**
**English Grammar for Students of Italian**
**English Grammar for Students of Latin**
**English Grammar for Students of Russian**



Printed in the U.S.A.

Library of Congress Catalog Card Number: 82-80514

ISBN 0-934034-03-6

10 9 8 7

## Contents

## Preface

*English Grammar for Students of Latin* is a handbook written in simple English to help students in elementary Latin classes understand the basic grammatical concepts of both languages. It is based on the similar handbooks published in a series: *English Grammar for Students of French* by Jacqueline Morton, *English Grammar for Students of Spanish* by Emily Spinelli, *English Grammar for Students of German* by Cecile Zorach, and *English Grammar for Students of Italian* by Sergio Adorni and Karen Primorac. Jacqueline Morton has edited the entire series.

The familiar and frustrating problem for both Latin teachers and students is that the language textbook assumes a knowledge of grammatical concepts, case for nouns and tense for verbs, along with conjugational patterns, on the part of students. Unfortunately, more and more students come to the classroom today with a limited background in understanding these ideas. The foreign language teacher, therefore, spends much valuable time in class teaching the basic English grammar that must precede teaching the same idea in the foreign language. When English speaking students use their own language, they do not have to analyze the difference between the direct and the indirect object, they do not have to name the parts of speech, for they are using the words in patterns that they have learned orally. When faced with the problem of analyzing the structure of the sentence, recognizing parts of speech, and the subtle ways in which nouns, verbs, and adjectives change endings in the foreign language, the student is bewildered by the new territory into which he is led and the lack of familiar signposts.

This book does not attempt to act as a substitute for the Latin textbook. Indeed, after learning the grammatical concept in the handbook, the student is referred to his Latin textbook for a complete declension or conjugation. The handbook should help the teacher and the student make the most efficient use of the classroom time and the classroom text. The handbook assumes no knowledge of grammar at all, and it tries to explain, in the most simple English, the complexities of English grammar and the Latin equivalents. We have tried to use example sentences from mythology to make the sentences lively and interesting. If the myth is too complex to be obvious in the example sentence, a footnote explains the story or the teacher may wish to elaborate.

The grammar concepts have been correlated with several beginning textbooks so that all the material in a first year text is covered, even such complex ideas as the gerund and the gerundive. The handbook is designed so that each segment, written as an answer to a question, e.g., What is Meant by Gender?, can be consulted independently. The teacher can refer a student to the relevant section if "gender" is not clear after the rest of the class has mastered the concept. If, however, the entire class is puzzled by the choice of *who* or *whom* as object of a dangling preposition, then the whole class would profit from consulting the materials together.

Experience with the other texts of the series has shown that the handbook is most useful when a particular section is assigned as a supplement to the correlative lesson in the classroom textbook or to reinforce grammatical explanations given in class.

We wish to thank Jacqueline Morton for her critical editing of this fifth in the series of English Grammar texts and Ernest Ament for his encouragement and tangible support. We also thank Tatiana Cizevska for her valuable criticism and advice from pre-publication classroom use of sections of the book.

Norma Goldman
Ladislas Szymanski

# Introduction

Learning a foreign language, in this case Latin, requires that you look at each word in three ways:

1. The MEANING of the word. An English word must be connected with a Latin word which has an equivalent meaning.

   The English word *girl* has the same meaning as the Latin word **puella.**

   Words with equivalent meanings are learned by memorizing vocabulary items. Because so many English words come from Latin, it is often your knowledge of English that will help you memorize Latin words. Sometimes words with the same or related meaning are very similar in English and Latin. The meanings of Latin words with English derivatives are easy to learn:

| Latin | Meaning | English Derivative |
|---|---|---|
| fīlius | son | filial |
| īnsula | island | insulate |
| fāma | fame | fame |

*Son* has the same meaning as the Latin word **fīlius.** The English word *filial,* as in "filial love" (the love of a child for a parent), will help you associate the two. Try to find English words derived from the Latin words. The extra time will be well spent, for you will remember the Latin more easily, and you will also enrich your English vocabulary.

Occasionally knowing one Latin word will help you learn another.

Knowing that **fīlius** is *son* will help you learn that **fīlia** is *daughter*.

**Fīlius** and *filial* are called COGNATES, that is, words related to each other because they are based on a common stem or root.[1]

Sometimes there is little similarity between Latin words, and knowing one will not help you learn another. Therefore, you will have to learn each vocabulary item separately.

> Knowing that **fēmina** is *woman* will not help you learn that **vir** is *man.*

In addition to vocabulary items, you must also learn IDIOMS. These are expressions which are unique to a language; it is a language's particular way of expressing something. It is not the meaning of the individual word, or words, which is important, but the overall meaning. Words in combination take on a special meaning. For instance, to say "thank you" Latin uses equivalent expressions.

Tibi grātiās habeō.

Literally: I have thanks or gratitude to you.

*or*

Tibi grātiās agō.

Literally: I do thanks or gratitude to you.

Note also how Latin says "Goodbye."

Valē.

Literally: Be well.
Compare to our expression "Fare thee well."

---

[1]Many words in related languages are cognate. For instance, there are many cognates in the Romance languages, so-called because they are all descended from Latin, the language of the Romans. Compare the cognate words derived from **fīlius** (Latin): *fils* (French), *figlio* (Italian), *hijo* (Spanish), *filho* (Portuguese) and *fiu* (Romanian).

2. The CLASS of the word. Words are grouped by types, each type being called a PART OF SPEECH. Depending on its part of speech, a word will follow certain rules. You must learn to identify the parts of speech in meeting words in the vocabulary and in sentences so that you will know what rules to apply.

There are eight different parts of speech:

| | |
|---|---|
| noun | verb |
| pronoun | adverb |
| adjective | preposition |
| conjunction | interjection |

Each part of speech has its own rules for use. This handbook will teach you to recognize the parts of speech in order to choose the correct Latin equivalent and to use the words correctly in sentences. Look at the word *love* in the following sentences:

The students *love* to learn the language.
(*love* — verb)

My *love* is like a red, red rose.
(*love* — noun)

He is famous for writing *love* stories.
(*love* — adjective)

In English the word is the same, but in Latin three different words, each following a different set of rules, must be used because each *love* belongs to a different part of speech.

3. The USE of the word. In addition to its class as a part of speech, a word must be identified according to the role it plays in the sentence. Each word, whether English or Latin, serves a unique function within the sentence. Determining the use or function of a word will help you use it properly in English and will help you find the proper Latin equivalent. Look at the word *her* in the following sentences:

All the students admire *her*.
direct object

The teacher gave *her* an "A."
indirect object

Are you going to graduate with *her?*
object of preposition *with*

*Her* work is excellent.
adjective

In English the word is the same in all four sentences, but in Latin the word will be different in each sentence, because the word *her* has four different uses.

**Nota Bene**[1]: As a student of Latin you must learn to recognize the parts of speech and the function of the words within the sentence, for the words have great influence on each other. Compare this sentence in English and in Latin:

*The beautiful small* ***islands*** *are in the large Mediterranean Sea.*

Parvae **īnsulae** pulchrae sunt in magnō **marī** Mediterrāneō.

**In English:** The only word that affects another is ***islands,*** which affects *are.* If the word were *island,* the verb *are* would be *is.*

**In Latin:** The word for *islands* (**īnsulae**) affects not only *are* (**sunt**), but also the words for *beautiful* (**pulchrae**) and *small* (**parvae**). The word for *sea* (**marī**) affects the equivalent words for *large* (**magnō**) and *Mediterranean* (**Mediterrāneō**). The only word unaffected by the other words is the preposition *in* (**in**), but it affects the word *sea* (**marī**).

[1]**Notā Bene:** *note well,* abbreviated N.B.

Since parts of speech and their use are usually determined in the same way in all the Romance languages (French, Spanish, Portuguese, Italian, and Romanian), as well as in Latin and English, this handbook will be of great value in showing you how to determine the parts of speech in many languages. This ability will give you a control of the grammar in your own English language as well as in Latin.

## What is a Noun?

A NOUN is a word that can be the name of:

| | |
|---|---|
| • a person | girl, teacher, god, Minerva, Jupiter |
| • a place | island, city, state, country, Rome, Italy |
| • a thing or animal | map, sea, picture, star, island, bull, Cerberus (dog of the Underworld) |
| • an idea | peace, war, democracy, love, virtue, luxury |

**In English:** Nouns that always begin with a capital letter, such as the names of people and places (Jupiter, Minerva, Italy, Rome) are called PROPER NOUNS. Nouns that do not begin with a capital letter (peace, love, professor, dog) are called COMMON NOUNS. A COMPOUND NOUN consists of two words (North Africa). To help you recognize nouns, here is a paragraph where the nouns are in italics.

The ***Romans,*** at the ***time*** of the ***Empire,*** imported luxury[1] ***goods*** from ***countries*** around the ***Mediterranean Sea.*** A ***Roman*** could go from ***England*** to ***Asia Minor*** without ***crossing***[2] a national ***boundary***; all the ***goods*** from the various ***regions*** were imported into ***Rome*** to satisfy the ***taste*** for elegant ***living***: ***oysters*** from ***England***, special ***wines*** from ***Spain***, ***animals*** for the gladiatorial ***games*** in the great ***amphitheaters*** from ***North Africa***, dried ***fruits, nuts, lumber, metals,*** and purple-dyed ***cloth*** from the ***Near East.*** Fancy inlaid ***furniture*** manufactured in ***Asia Minor*** decorated the ***rooms*** of the wealthy ***Romans***, while Greek ***statues*** and finely painted ***vases*** decorated the ***garden*** and ***atrium. Spices*** for ***foods*** and ***medicines*** made up a great ***market*** in ***Rome***, and ***marble*** in various ***colors*** was imported to decorate the ***temples***. The unfavorable ***balance*** of ***trade*** was so serious a ***problem*** under the ***Emperor Vespasian*** that he set up a special ***investigation*** to find out why ***Rome*** was sending out so much ***money*** for ***imports.***

**In Latin:** Nouns generally have the same function that they have in English.

---

[1]This is an example of a noun used as an adjective.

[2]*Crossing* is a verbal noun, object of the preposition *without* (see **What is a Verbal Noun (a Gerund)?**, p. 90).

## What is Meant by Gender?

**GENDER** is the classification of a word as masculine, feminine, or neuter.

Gender plays an obvious role in English; however in Latin it is not always so obvious. First let us see what evidence we have of gender in English.

**In English:** We often use a noun without realizing that it has gender. However, when we replace the noun with the pronoun *he, she,* or *it,* we choose one of these three without hesitation because we automatically give the gender to the noun we are replacing.

- The ***boy*** came home; ***he*** was tired, and I was glad to see ***him.***

  A noun (*boy*) is **MASCULINE GENDER** if *he* or *him* is used to substitute for the noun.

- My ***aunt*** came for a visit; ***she*** is kind and I like ***her.***

  A noun (*aunt*) is **FEMININE GENDER** if *she* or *her* is used to substitute for the noun.

- There is a ***tree*** in front of the house. ***It*** is a maple.

  A noun (*tree*) is **NEUTER GENDER** if *it* is substituted for the noun.

**In Latin:** All nouns, common and proper, are either masculine, feminine, or neuter. The gender of Latin nouns is either natural or grammatical. **NATURAL GENDER** is distinction as to the sex of the object. **GRAMMATICAL GENDER** is a distinction as to sex where no actual sex exists in the object. Perhaps these sex designations stem from ancient ideas that inanimate objects had male or female functions, such as the earth being the reproductive mother: **terra** (*earth*) is feminine.

1. natural gender—based on the sex of the noun

   - all words referring to males are masculine

| | |
|---|---|
| deus | *god* |
| Iuppiter | *Jupiter* |
| puer | *boy* |

   - all words referring to females are feminine

| | |
|---|---|
| māter | *mother* |
| fīlia | *daughter* |
| rēgīna | *queen* |

   - some nouns referring to things are neuter

| | |
|---|---|
| templum | *temple* |
| dōnum | *gift* |
| cornū | *horn* |

2. grammatical gender—sex designation where no actual sex exists

   Many nouns that are neuter in English (objects, countries, rivers, cities, etc.) are either masculine or feminine, although some are neuter.[1]

| Examples of English nouns whose equivalents are MASCULINE in Latin | Examples of English nouns whose equivalents are FEMININE in Latin | Examples of English nouns whose equivalents are NEUTER in Latin |
|---|---|---|
| book | boat | river |
| chariot | tree | temple |
| army | courage | gift |
| field | country | animal |
| mountain | Athens | example |
| foot | Rome | horn |

[1]In English we do refer to a car or a boat as "she" in a sentence like: "She is a great car." "The Queen Elizabeth is in dock. She is a fine ship." We can thus understand this phenomenon called grammatical gender.

With each new noun it is important to memorize its gender. This gender is important for the noun itself, and also for the gender of words which it influences: pronouns, adjectives and participles.

Gender can sometimes be determined by looking at the ending of the first form of a Latin noun as given in your vocabulary. Below are some noun endings which often correspond to the masculine, feminine, or neuter genders. Since you will see these endings frequently, it is worth being familiar with them, although exceptions do occur.

## Masculine endings

| | |
|---|---|
| **-us** | taurus (*bull*), amīcus (*friend*), Nīlus (*Nile*), Aegyptus (*Egypt*), animus (*soul*) |
| **-er** | puer (*boy*), ager (*field*), Iuppiter (*Jupiter*), pater (*father*) |
| **-or** | auctor (*author*), ōrātor (*orator*), victor (*victor*), amor (*love*) |

## Feminine endings

| | |
|---|---|
| **-a** | puella (*girl*), fēmina (*woman*), porta (*gate*), glōria (*glory*) |
| **-ās** | vānitās (*vanity*), aetās (*age*), vēritās (*truth*) |
| **-dō** | magnitūdō (*great size*), fortitūdō (*strength*), servitūdō (*slavery*) |
| **-iō** | regiō (*region*), actiō (*action*), religiō (*religion*), nōtiō (*notion*) |

## Neuter endings

| | |
|---|---|
| **-um** | templum (*temple*), pōmum (*apple*), dōnum (*gift*) |
| **-men** | flūmen (*river*), agmen (*line of battle*), nōmen (*name*) |
| **-e** | mare (*sea*) |
| **-al** | animal (*animal*) |
| **-ar** | exemplar (*example*) |

It is also helpful to know that names of rivers, winds, months and mountains are masculine. Names of cities, countries, plants, trees, and most abstract qualities are feminine.

## What is Meant by Number?

**NUMBER** is the indication of a word as singular or plural. When a word refers to one person or thing, it is said to be **SINGULAR**, when it refers to more than one, it is called **PLURAL**. Not all parts of speech can have a singular and plural, only nouns, pronouns, adjectives (in Latin) and verbs. The plural of a word is formed according to different rules, depending on the part of speech to which it belongs. In this section let us explain the plural of nouns (see **What is a Noun?**, p. 5).

**In English:** A singular noun is made plural in several ways:

- by adding an ***-s*** or ***-es*** to the singular noun

| | | |
|---|---|---|
| book | ⟶ | books |
| kiss | ⟶ | kisses |

- by making a spelling change or addition

| | | |
|---|---|---|
| man | ⟶ | men |
| mouse | ⟶ | mice |
| leaf | ⟶ | leaves |
| child | ⟶ | children |

A plural noun is usually spelled differently and pronounced differently from the singular.

Some nouns, called **COLLECTIVE NOUNS**, refer to a group of persons or things, but they are considered singular.

A football *team* has eleven players.
The *family* is all here now.
The *crowd* was under control.

**In Latin:** A singular noun is usually made plural by having its ending changed, although there are words that change internally as well.

| | | | |
|---|---|---|---|
| puell**a** → puell**ae** | | *girl* → *girls* | |
| am**ī**c**us** → am**ī**c**ī** | | *friend* → *friends* | |
| templ**um** → templ**a** | | *temple* → *temples* | |
| pat**er** → patr**ēs** | | *father* → *fathers* | |
| op**us** → op**era** | | *work* → *works* | |

N.B.: Nouns do not change gender when they become plural.

There are patterns to help you to form the plural of Latin nouns. To help you remember the patterns, here are examples using Latin words commonly used in English. You might note that when the words are used in English, the Latin form of the plural is preferred (alternate English spellings are indicated in parentheses).

- most singular feminine nouns change the ending **-a** to **-ae**

| | | |
|---|---|---|
| alumn**a** | *girl graduate* | alumn**ae** |
| antenn**a** | *feeler on an insect* | antenn**ae** (*antennas is used for television aerials)* |

- most masculine nouns change the ending **-us** to **-i**

| | | |
|---|---|---|
| alumn**us** | *male graduate* | alumn**ī** |
| gladiol**us** | *the flower* | gladiol**ī** (*gladioluses*) |

- most neuter nouns change the ending **-um** to **-a**

| | | |
|---|---|---|
| dat**um** *something given* | | dat**a** |
| curricul**um** | | curricul**a** (*curriculums*) |
| stadi**um** | | stadi**a** (*stadiums*) |

- a few words that end in **-ex** or **-ix** change to **-icēs**

| | |
|---|---|
| ind**ex** | ind**icēs** (*indexes*) |
| append**ix** | append**icēs** (*appendixes*) |

Collective nouns generally use a singular verb to agree with a singular collective noun.

Populus Rōmānus **est** bonus.
singular (Populus) — singular (est)

*The Roman people* ***are*** *good.*
singular (people) — plural (are)

## What are Indefinite and Definite Articles?

The ARTICLE is a word which is placed before a noun to show if the noun refers to a particular person, place, thing, animal or idea, or if the noun refers to an unspecified person, place, thing, animal or idea.[1]

**In English:** The indefinite article ***a*** or ***an*** is placed before a noun to show that the noun does not refer to a particular person, place, thing, animal or idea.

- use ***a*** before a word beginning with a consonant

  I saw *a* boy in the street.
  not a particular boy

- use ***an*** before a word beginning with a vowel

  I ate *an* apple.
  not a particular apple

[1]Since the article modifies a noun, it is considered an adjective (see **What is an Adjective?**, p. 130).

The definite article ***the*** is placed before the noun if it refers to a specific person, place, thing, animal or idea.

I saw *the* boy in the street.
a specific boy

I ate *the* apple.
a specific apple

**In Latin:** There are no articles, and when a Latin sentence is translated into English, the article must be added, if necessary. Your knowledge of English and the meaning of the sentence will help you supply the correct article (*a, an,* or *the*), the one which best suits the meaning of the sentence or paragraph; or omit the article entirely.

- Puella in casā habitat.
  girl house

  ***The** girl lives in **a** house.*

- Mīlitēs nōn semper sunt fortēs.
  soldiers

  *Soldiers are not always brave.*

## What is Meant by Case?

CASE is the change in the form of a word to show how it functions within the sentence. This change of form usually takes place in the ending of the word; sometimes, however, the entire word changes.

**In English:** The order of words in the sentence signals the function of the nouns and hence shows the meaning of the whole sentence. We easily recognize the difference in meaning between the following two sentences purely on the basis of word order. The nouns themselves remain the same even though they serve different functions in each sentence.

The girl sees the bull on the shore.

Here *the girl* is seeing, and *the bull* is what she sees.

The bull sees the girl on the shore.

Here *the bull* is seeing, and *the girl* is whom it sees.

The words for *girl* and *bull* are spelled the same whatever their function in the sentence. It is the word order that indicates the meaning of the sentence.

The term NOMINATIVE CASE or SUBJECTIVE CASE is used for the person or thing doing the action of the verb: *girl* in the first sentence because she is doing the seeing; *bull* in the second sentence.

The term OBJECTIVE CASE is used for the person or thing receiving the action of the verb: *bull* in the first sentence because it is what the girl sees; *girl* in the second sentence because it is what (whom) the bull sees.

In English there is a third case called the POSSESSIVE CASE which indicates ownership.

The girl sees the *farmer's* bull on the shore.

The farmer is the person who owns the bull, and the ownership is indicated by *'s* added to *the farmer* (see **What is the Possessive?**, p. 29).

In English we can see change of case with pronouns (see **What is a Personal Pronoun?**, p. 40). In the two examples below, it is not just the word order but also the form, i.e. the case, of the pronoun which affects the meaning of the sentence.

I know *them.*

They know *me.*

We cannot say, "I know *they*" or "They know *I*" because the forms "they" and "I" cannot be used as objects of a verb (see **What are Objects?**, p. 31). If you can recognize the different cases of pronouns in English, you may find it easier to understand the Latin case system.

English pronouns have three cases:

1. nominative: used for subjects and predicate words (see **What is a Subject?**, p. 24 and **What is a Predicate Word?**, p. 27).

   *He* and *I* went to the city.
   subjects = nominative case

   *We* enjoyed the sights.
   subject = nominative case

2. objective: used for direct objects, indirect objects, and objects of prepositions (see **What are Objects?**, p. 31).

   *They* invited both *him* and *me.*
   *They*: subject = nominative case
   *him* and *me*: direct object = objective case

*They* sent *us* a note.

subject = nominative | indirect object = objective

*We* asked about *them*.

subject = nominative | object of preposition = objective

*They* spoke to *her*.

subject = nominative | object of preposition = objective

In these examples the pronouns have different forms depending on how they are used in the sentence. The different cases prevent us from saying "Us went to the theater" or "Him talked about she."

3. possessive: used to show ownership; the possessive pronoun can function as subject, predicate noun, direct object, indirect object, or object of preposition.

This book is *yours*.

possessive pronoun = predicate word

John called his parents, but I wrote *mine* a letter.

possessive pronoun = indirect object

Mary has finished her test, but John is still working on *his*.

possessive pronoun = object of preposition

The possessive case is discussed in a separate section (see **What is a Possessive Pronoun?**, p. 172).

**In Latin:** Word order alone rarely shows the function of nouns within the sentence. Instead, the different endings of the Latin nouns indicate the change called case. As long as the nouns are put in their proper case, the words in the sentence can be moved around in a variety of ways without changing the essential meaning of the sentence.

Look at the many ways the following sentence can be expressed in Latin:

*The girl sees the bull on the shore.*[1]

- | Puella | taurum | in rīpā | videt. |
  |---|---|---|---|
  | nom. = subject | acc. = direct object | obj. of prep. | |
  | *girl* | *bull* | *on shore* | *sees* |

- | Taurum | in rīpā | puella | videt. |
  |---|---|---|---|
  | acc. = direct object | obj. of prep. | nom. = subject | |
  | *bull* | *on shore* | *girl* | *sees* |

  Since *bull* is being emphasized by its first position, this sentence means that the girl sees the bull and not some other creature.

- | In rīpā | taurum | puella | videt. |
  |---|---|---|---|
  | obj. of prep. | acc.= direct object | nom. = subject | |
  | *on shore* | *bull* | *girl* | *sees* |

  Since *on the shore* is being emphasized by its first position, this sentence means that the girl sees the bull on the shore and not somewhere else.

---

[1]The god Jupiter fell in love with the maiden Europa and came to earth in the form of a bull. After the bull had enticed the girl onto his back, he travelled across the sea with her to Crete.

Because of the case endings, it is evident that the *girl* (**puella**—nominative—in all three sentences) is doing the looking and that the *bull* (**taurum**—accusative—in all three sentences) is what the girl sees. The different word order simply shows what the writer wants to stress. The case endings indicate the function and relationship of words to each other.

Latin nouns, pronouns and adjectives have five main cases, each with singular and plural forms, usually indicated by a change of ending. All these possible forms are called a DECLENSION. Here is the name of each case:

1. nominative (subjective case)—first form listed in your vocabulary
2. genitive (possessive case—sometimes objective case)
3. dative }
4. accusative } (objective case)
5. ablative }

The different cases are used as follows:

1. The NOMINATIVE CASE is used for the subject of the sentence and for predicate words. (See **What is a Subject?**, p. 24, and **What is a Predicate Word?**, p. 27.)

2. The GENITIVE CASE is used to show possession. (See **What is the Possessive?**, p. 29.) Sometimes it is used as an object (see p. 30).

3. The DATIVE CASE is used for indirect objects and for the objects of a few verbs. (See **What are Objects?**, p. 31.)

4. The ACCUSATIVE CASE is used for most direct objects and as object of certain prepositions. (See **What are Objects?**, p. 31, and **What is a Preposition?**, p. 187.)

5. The ABLATIVE CASE is used for the object of certain prepositions and for adverbial expressions. (See **What are Objects?**, p. 31, and **What is an Adverb?**, p. 158.)

Memorizing these 10 forms (5 singular and 5 plural) for all nouns, pronouns and adjectives is made easy by the Latin system of declensions. Fortunately, most Latin words are declined according to one of five patterns: **FIRST DECLENSION, SECOND DECLENSION, THIRD DECLENSION, FOURTH DECLENSION,** and **FIFTH DECLENSION.** You must memorize one sample for each declension, and the same pattern can be applied to all other words in the same group or declension.

When you learn the nominative of a new noun or adjective, you must also memorize its genitive singular form because it gives you two essential facts:

1. The genitive singular ending enables you to identify the declension to which each word belongs.

   Here is a list of the genitive singular endings for each declension.

| Declension | Genitive singular ending | Nominative | Genitive singular | |
|---|---|---|---|---|
| 1st | **-ae** | silva | silv**ae** | *forest* |
| 2nd | **-ī** | animus | anim**ī** | *soul, mind* |
| 3rd | **-is** | rēx | rēg**is** | *king* |
| 4th | **-ūs** | exercitus | exercit**ūs** | *army* |
| 5th | **-eī** | fidēs | fid**eī** | *faith* |

2. The genitive singular provides you with the stem to which the endings for each declension are attached. To find this stem, merely drop the genitive ending (see above chart) from the genitive singular form. Here is an example for each declension.

| Declension | Genitive singular | Stem |
|---|---|---|
| 1st | silv**ae** | silv- |
| 2nd | anim**ī** | anim- |
| 3rd | rēg**is** | rēg- |
| 4th | exercit**ūs** | exercit- |
| 5th | fid**eī** | fid- |

It is particularly important to establish this stem with nouns belonging to the third declension because the genitive singular is often substantially different from the nominative singular. For example,

virgo, virginis, *f. maiden*

Applying the same formula, one drops the **-is** ending of the genitive singular and uses the stem **virgin-** to which the endings of the third declension are added. Consult your textbook for these endings.

The English derivatives of many Latin nouns are based on the genitive singular stem of these nouns and should help you remember the form.

| Nominative singular | | Genitive singular | English derivative |
|---|---|---|---|
| nōmen | *name* | **nōmin**is | *nomin*ate |
| rēx | *king* | **rēg**is | *reg*al |
| virgō | *maiden* | **virgin**is | *virgin, virgin*al |

Remember: Learn the genitive singular with each noun to determine the stem onto which the various case endings will be added. Consult your Latin textbook for the endings which are to be added to these stems to indicate case and number in all five declensions.

There are a few nouns that are irregular in that they do not follow a specific declension, but take endings from several declensions. Your textbook will identify them and you will have to learn them individually.

Since the learning of declensions is so important for a beginning Latin student, let us go over a sample of a noun of the first declension. The principle will be the same for the other four declensions.

The word is listed in your vocabulary as **silva, -ae,** *f. forest.* The first form is the nominative singular; the second **-ae** is the genitive singular ending which must be attached to the stem; and the *f.* stands for the gender, feminine.

- **silva, silvae,** *f. forest*

1. Find the stem—take the genitive singular form and drop the ending:

   **silv**-ae

2. Add the endings of the first declension—listed in your textbook:

| Case | Singular | Plural |
|---|---|---|
| Nominative | **-a** | **-ae** |
| Genitive | **-ae** | **-ārum** |
| Dative | **-ae** | **-īs** |
| Accusative | **-am** | **-ās** |
| Ablative | **-ā** | **-īs** |

Thus, the declension of the word **silva** reads as follows:

| | Singular | Plural | Usage |
|---|---|---|---|
| Nominative | silva | silvae | *subject or predicate word* |
| Genitive | silvae | silvārum | *possession* |
| Dative | silvae | silvīs | *indirect object* |
| Accusative | silvam | silvās | *direct object or object of preposition* |
| Ablative | silvā | silvīs | *object of preposition or adverbial expressions* |

Notice that the **-ā** of the ablative singular ending has a long mark called a MACRON over it, indicating that it is a long vowel. It is important to mark the long **-ā** of the ablative singular to differentiate it from the short **-a** of the nominative singular ending.[1]

You can apply this same pattern for all of the nouns of the first declension and for adjectives which modify them.

Once you have established the correct forms of the declension of a particular word, you must decide which case to use in the Latin sentence. Here are a series of steps you should follow:

*The girls give the bull flowers.*

1. Identify the gender and number of each noun.

| | |
|---|---|
| girls: | **Puellae** is feminine plural. |
| bull: | **Taurō** is masculine singular. |
| flowers: | **Flōrēs** is masculine plural. |

2. Determine how each noun functions in the sentence.

| | | |
|---|---|---|
| girls | = | subject |
| bull | = | indirect object |
| flowers | = | direct object |

3. Determine what case in Latin corresponds to the function you have identified in step 2.

| | | | | |
|---|---|---|---|---|
| girls | = | subject | ——• | nominative case |
| bull | = | indirect object | ——• | dative case |
| flowers | = | direct object | ——• | accusative case |

[1]Vowels in Latin are either long or short. The long ones are marked with the macron or long mark, indicating the length of time they are held and how they are pronounced. The Romans did not use the long marks, since they knew how to pronounce their words. We do not need to have marks in English to tell us how to pronounce *cat* (short *a*) or *Kate* (long *a*). Listen to how much longer the *a* in Kate is held. In Latin the long **-a-** is merely held longer, but is not changed in sound. The other vowels are both held longer and sounded differently. Listen to the pronunciation of words in class, and your teacher will give the rules for the length of vowels with the chart provided in your textbook. Your best guide is to imitate the correct pronunciation of words in class. It is important to mark the long **a** of the ablative singular to distinguish it from the nominative singular. Your teacher may or may not insist that you mark the long vowels in the other endings.

4. Choose the proper form from those which you have memorized.

| Puellae | taurō | flōrēs | dant. |
|---|---|---|---|
| \| | \| | \| | |
| nom. | dat. | acc. | |
| fem. | masc. | masc. | |
| pl. | sing. | pl. | |

Notice how changing the function of a word in a Latin sentence requires changing its case as well.

*The bull gives the girls flowers.*

| Taurus | puellīs | flōrēs | dat. |
|---|---|---|---|
| \| | \| | \| | |
| nom. | dat. | acc. | |
| masc. | fem. | masc. | |
| sing. | pl. | pl. | |

There are two other cases in Latin whose endings, for the most part, are similar to the endings of other cases:

- The **VOCATIVE CASE** is used for the name of the person or persons who are being spoken to. The endings are very similar to the nominative differing only in the masculine singular of the second declension. Consult your textbook for the various forms.

  **Eurōpa**, cavē taurum!
  ***Europa,*** *beware of the bull!*

  **Domine,** fīlia tua rapta est!
  ***Master,*** *your daughter has been carried off.*

- The **LOCATIVE CASE** is used for the noun indicating the location of someone or something. (See **What is a Preposition?**, p. 187.)

  Eurōpa cum patre **domī** habitābat.
  *Europa lived* ***at home*** *with her father.*

Agricolae **rūrī** laborant.
*Farmers work **in the country.***

## What is a Subject?

The SUBJECT of a sentence is the person or thing that performs the action of the verb.[1] When you wish to find the subject of a sentence, always look for the verb first; then ask, *WHO?* OR *WHAT?* BEFORE THE VERB. The answer will be the subject.

- The goddess talks to the woman.

  ***Who*** talks to the woman?
  Answer: the goddess.

  *The goddess* is the singular subject.

- Apollo and Diana are the children of the goddess.

  ***Who*** are the children of the goddess?
  Answer: Apollo and Diana.

  *Apollo and Diana* is the plural subject.

- Did the women listen to the goddess?

  ***Who*** did listen to the goddess?
  Answer: the women.

  *The women* is the plural subject.

---

[1]The subject performs the action in the active sentence, but is acted upon in a passive sentence (see **What is Meant by Active and Passive Voice?**, p. 93).

Train yourself to ask the question to find the subject. Never assume that a word is the subject because it comes first in the sentence.

Subjects can be in many different places of a sentence, as you can see in the following examples in which the subject is in boldface and the verb is italicized.

> After listening to his mother, ***Apollo*** *killed* the sons of the queen.[1]
> *Did* ***Apollo*** *kill* all the sons of the queen?
> Grieving the loss of her children, all alone *stood* ***Niobe.***

Subject words are often referred to as being in the SUBJECTIVE CASE (see p. 14).

Some sentences have more than one main verb; you have to find the subject of each verb.

> ***Latona*** *calls* her children, and ***they*** *kill* the sons and daughters of Niobe.

*Latona* is the singular subject of the first verb *calls,* and *they* is the plural subject of the second verb *kill.*

In both English and Latin it is very important to find the subject of each verb to make sure that the subject and the verb agree: that is, you must choose the form of the verb which is singular to agree with a singular subject; if the subject is plural, the verb must be plural. (See **What is a Verb Conjugation?**, p. 58.)

**In Latin:** It is particularly important that you recognize the subject of a sentence so that you will put it in the proper case (see **What is Meant by Case?**, p. 14). The subject of a Latin sentence is in the nominative case.

---

[1]Niobe had boasted about her seven sons and seven daughters, asking the women of the town to pray to her and not to the goddess Latona, who only had one son and daughter, Apollo and Diana. The goddess, enraged, sent her powerful children to kill the sons and daughters of Niobe.

- **Iuppiter** Eurōpam amat.

  noun — verb

  nom. masc. sing. — 3rd person sing.

  ***Jupiter** loves Europa.*

- **Puerī** puellās pulchrās amant.

  nom. masc. pl. — 3rd person pl.

  ***The boys** love the beautiful girls.*

- **Minerva** bene labōrat.

  nom. fem. sing. — 3rd person sing.

  ***Minerva** works well.*

- **Nymphae** pictūram pulchram amant.

  nom. fem. pl. — 3rd person pl.

  ***The nymphs** like the beautiful picture.*

- **Templum** est pulchrum.

  nom. neut. sing. — 3rd person sing.

  ***The temple** is beautiful.*

- **Dōna** pulchra sunt deae grāta.

  nom. neut. pl. — 3rd person pl.

  *Beautiful **gifts** are pleasing to the goddess.*

## What is a Predicate Word?

A **PREDICATE WORD** is one which defines or describes the sentence's subject and which is connected to the subject by a linking verb. A **LINKING VERB** is an intransitive verb (see p. 51) which connects or *links* the predicate word (noun, pronoun, or adjective) back to the subject.

**In English:** Some common linking verbs in English are the verbs ***to be** (is, are)*, ***to seem, to appear, to become.*** Although these verbs often have nouns, pronouns or adjectives following them, the nouns, pronouns or adjectives are not direct objects (see **What are Objects?**, p. 31), but predicate words. Learn to look for them following linking verbs. They refer back to the subject.

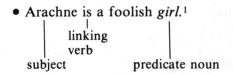

- Arachne is a foolish *girl.*[1]

  Arachne → subject; is → linking verb; girl → predicate noun

- Fools are *those* who challenge the gods.

  Fools → subject; are → linking verb; those → predicate pronoun

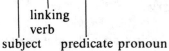

- Minerva becomes *angry.*

  Minerva → subject; becomes → linking verb; angry → predicate adjective

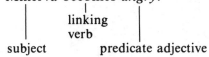

**In Latin:** Predicate words are in the same case as the subject (see **What is Meant by Case?**, p. 14). Observe how the predicate words in the following sentences refer back to the subject, which is also in the nominative case.

---

[1]Arachne was a skillful weaver who challenged the goddess Minerva to a weaving contest. The goddess, enraged that the girl was so presumptuous, changed her into a spider.

- Arachnē est **puella** stulta.

  linking verb

  subject predicate noun

  nom. sing. fem.

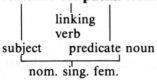

  *Arachne is a foolish **girl.***

- Hominēs stultī sunt **illī** quī deōs prōvocant.

  linking verb

  subject predicate pronoun

  nom. pl. masc.

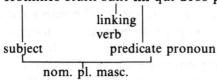

  *Fools are **those** who challenge the gods.*

- Minerva fit **īrāta.**

  linking verb

  subject predicate adjective

  nom. sing. fem.

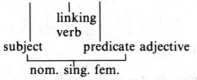

  *Minerva becomes **angry.***

Learn to recognize forms of the linking verbs like **esse** (*to be*), **fierī** (*to become*), and **vidērī** (*to seem*), which appear with predicate words.

## What is the Possessive?

The term **POSSESSIVE** means that one noun owns or *possesses* another noun.

**In English:** You can show possession in one of two ways:

1. with an *APOSTROPHE*

- by adding apostrophe "s" to a singular possessor noun

  the teacher's book
  Ovid's poetry
  the bird's song

- by adding an apostrophe to the plural possessor noun

  the girls' father
  the boys' mother

2. with the word *OF*

  the book *of* the teacher
  the poetry *of* Ovid
  the song *of* the bird

**In Latin:** Possession is shown by using the genitive case for the possessor, the noun that owns the other noun. The noun being possessed usually stands first in normal word order, but the endings make clear the relationship.

- liber **magistrī**

  nom. genitive sing.

  *the book* ***of the teacher*** (or ***the teacher's*** *book*)

- carmen **poētae**

  nom. genitive sing.

  *the song **of the poet*** (or ***the poet's** song*)

- pater **puellārum**

  nom. genitive pl.

  *the father **of the girls*** (or ***the girls'** father*)

- māter **puerōrum**

  nom. genitive pl.

  *the mother **of the boys*** (or ***the boys'** mother*)

There is no word in Latin for the word "of" in the sense of possession. **Casa puellae** can mean *the girl's house* or *the house of the girl.* Either translation is correct.

N.B. Not every use of the word "of" implies possession. The word "of" appears in another genitive usage called the **OBJECTIVE GENITIVE.**

- Amōrem **pecūniae** dēmōnstrābat.

  genitive sing.

  *He showed a love **of money.***

- Odium **meī** erat manifestum.

  genitive sing.

  *His hatred **of me** was clear.*

This usage is called the objective genitive because it is the same thing as saying "He loves money" or "He hates me."

## What are Objects?

**OBJECTS** are nouns or pronouns that receive the action of verbs or complete prepositional phrases. In order to be able to choose the correct case of nouns or pronouns, you must understand the difference between the various kinds of objects in both English and Latin. Let us examine the world of objects.

Most sentences consist, at the very least, of a subject and a verb.

Children play.
Work stopped.

The subject of the sentence is a noun or a pronoun. Most sentences, however, contain other nouns or pronouns. Many of these function as objects. These objects are divided into three categories, depending upon their position in the sentence and how they are used. The three types of objects are:

1. direct object
2. indirect object
3. object of a preposition

1. Direct object and 2. Indirect object

**In English:**

1. **DIRECT OBJECT:** The direct object receives the action of the verb directly, without prepositions separating the verb from the receiver. It answers the ONE-WORD QUESTION *WHAT?* OR *WHOM?* ASKED AFTER THE VERB.

- The god loves ***the nymph.***

  The god loves *whom?* The nymph.
  *The nymph* is the direct object.

- The girl sees ***the bull.***

  The girl sees *what?* The bull.
  *The bull* is the direct object.

Object words are often referred to as being in the objective case (see p. 14). Never assume that a word is the direct object. Always ask the one-word question, and if you do not get an answer, you do not have a direct object in the sentence. Some sentences do not have direct objects.

- The girls work well.

  The girls work *what?* Nothing, no answer possible.
  The girls work *whom?* No one, no answer possible.

  This sentence has no direct object. *Well* is an adverb telling how the girls worked.

2. INDIRECT OBJECT: The indirect object also receives the action of the verb, but it receives the action indirectly; it explains "to whom" or "for whom," or "to what" or "for what" the action of the verb is done. It answers the TWO-WORD QUESTION *TO WHOM/FOR WHOM* OR *TO WHAT/FOR WHAT* ASKED AFTER THE VERB.[1]

- The boy writes his mother.

  The boy writes *to whom?* To his mother.
  *His mother* is the indirect object.

- The farmer did me a favor.

  The farmer did a favor *for whom?* For me.
  *Me* is the indirect object.

**In Latin:** Objects are divided into categories depending on their case. The accusative case is used for the direct object and the dative is used for the indirect object.

1. Direct object: Most English direct objects are in the accusative case in Latin.

[1]Every use of *to* or *for* does not identify an indirect object. *To* and *for* can also introduce prepositional phrases of direction toward a location (see p. 191).

- *The god loves **the girl.***

  The god loves *whom?* The girl.
  *The girl* is the direct object.

  Deus **puellam** amat.

  direct object =
  accusative

- *The girl sees **the bull.***

  The girl sees *what?* The bull.
  *The bull* is the direct object.

  Puella **taurum** videt.

  direct object =
  accusative

Verbs generally take the accusative for the direct object, but some verbs take other cases. Consult your textbook for these exceptions.

2. Indirect object: Most English indirect objects are in the dative case in Latin.

- *The boy writes **to his mother.***

  The boy writes *to whom?* To his mother.
  *His mother* is the indirect object.

  Puer **mātrī** scrībit.

  indirect object =
  dative

- *Mark did **me** a favor.*

  Mark did a favor *for whom?* For me.
  *Me* is the indirect object.

  Marcus **mihi** grātum fēcit.

  indirect object =
  dative

A sentence may contain both a direct object and an indirect object.

**In English:** Many verbs in English have two objects. In the sentence the indirect object will usually come before the direct object, unless the indirect object is expanded to a prepositional phrase beginning with *to* (see p. 33).

- He brought his mother flowers. (He brought flowers to his mother.)
  - brought = verb; mother = indirect object; flowers = direct object

  He bought *what?* Flowers.
  *Flowers* is the direct object.

  He brought flowers *for whom?* For his mother.
  *His mother* is the indirect object.

- We gave the teacher a gift. (We gave a gift to the teacher.)
  - gave = verb; teacher = indirect object; gift = direct object

  We gave *what?* A gift.
  *A gift* is the direct object.

  We gave a gift *to whom?* To the teacher.
  *The teacher* is the indirect object.

**In Latin:** In a sentence with two objects you will need to determine which object is the direct object and which object is the indirect object. The direct object will be in the accusative case, and the indirect object will be in the dative case.

- *He brought **the goddess flowers.***
  - goddess = indirect object; flowers = direct object

  **Deae flōrēs** attulit.
  - Deae = ind. obj. = dative
  - flōrēs = dir. obj. = accusative

- We gave ***the teacher a gift.***

  indirect object (the teacher) — direct object (a gift)

**Magistrō dōnum** dedimus.

ind. obj. = dative (Magistrō)
dir. obj. = accusative (dōnum)

3. Object of preposition

**In English:** The noun or pronoun which follows the preposition is called the **OBJECT OF THE PREPOSITION**. The object of the preposition answers the TWO-WORD QUESTION made up of the PREPOSITION + *WHAT* OR *WHOM*.

- The tree is ***in the forest.***

  The tree is *in what?* In the forest.
  *Forest* is the object of the preposition *in*.

- Jupiter is walking ***with Mercury.***

  Jupiter is walking *with whom?* With Mercury.
  *Mercury* is the object of the preposition *with*.

There are many prepositions which take objects: *behind* the house, *out* the window, *without* him, *after* the war, *beside* the river, *before* the storm, *with* Diana, *inside* the palace, *over* the hill, *for* the emperor, *alongside* the road.

**In Latin:** The ablative or the accusative case is used for nouns or pronouns as objects of prepositions. Each preposition (see **What is a Preposition?**, p. 179) must be learned with its meaning and the case of the noun which follows it.

Let us first look at the ablative case used as object of the preposition.

- *The tree is **before the temple.***

  The tree is *before what?* Before the temple.
  *Temple* is the object of the preposition *before.*

  Arbor est **prō templō.**

  obj. of prep. **prō** + ablative

- *Jupiter is walking **with Mercury.***

  Jupiter is walking *with whom?* With Mercury.
  *Mercury* is the object of the preposition *with.*

  Iuppiter **cum Mercuriō** ambulat.

  obj. of prep. **cum** + ablative

Now let us see some prepositions that are followed by the accusative case.

- *The ship is sailing **to the island.***

  The ship is sailing *to what?* To the island.
  *Island* is the object of the preposition *to.*

  Nāvis **ad īnsulam** nāvigat.

  obj. of prep. **ad** + accusative

- *The bear wandered **through the woods.***

  The bear wandered *through what?* Through the woods.
  *Woods* is the object of the preposition *through.*

  Ursa **per silvam** errābat.

  obj. of prep. **per** + accusative

When you learn the meaning of the preposition be sure to learn also the case that follows it.

As a student of Latin you must watch out for some English verbs that are followed by a preposition and its object while the Latin equivalent verbs do not need a preposition and simply take a direct object in the accusative case.

- to look at—**spectāre** + accusative

  *The girls **are looking at** the stars.*
  Puellae stellās **spectant.**

  subject | direct object = accusative | verb

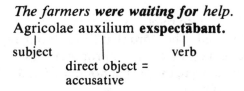

  The meaning of the verb **spectant** is "look at" and **stellās**, the "stars," is the direct object in the accusative case.

- to wait for—**exspectāre** + accusative

  *The farmers **were waiting for** help.*
  Agricolae auxilium **exspectābant.**

  subject | direct object = accusative | verb

  The meaning of the verb **exspectābant** is "were waiting for, were expecting" and **auxilium**, "help," is the direct object in the accusative case.

When you learn a Latin verb, be careful to notice whether it needs a preposition. With verbs like the ones above, the preposition is part of the English verb, but it is not necessary to be expressed in Latin.

## What is a Pronoun?

A **PRONOUN** is a word used in place of one or more nouns. It may stand, therefore, for a person, place, thing, or idea.

For instance, instead of repeating the proper noun "Midas" in the following sentences, it is more desirable to use a pronoun in the second sentence.

> *Midas* likes gold. *Midas* turns everything to gold.
> *Midas* likes gold. ***He*** turns everything to gold.

A pronoun can only be used to refer to something (or someone) that has already been mentioned. The word that the pronoun replaces or refers to is called the **ANTECEDENT** of the pronoun. In the example above, the pronoun *he* refers to the proper noun *Midas. Midas* is the antecedent of the pronoun *he.*

**In English:** There are different types of pronouns. They are studied in separate sections of this handbook. Listed below are the most important categories and the section where they are discussed in detail.

- **PERSONAL PRONOUNS**—These pronouns change in form in the different persons and according to the function they have in the sentence.

  - as subject (see p. 40)

    *I* go; *they* read; *he* runs; *she* sings.

  - as direct object (see p. 44)

    Midas loves *it.* Pan saw *her.* Apollo killed *them.*

  - as indirect object (see p. 44)

    The goddess gave *him* advice. Send *them* help. Give *her* gifts.

- as object of a preposition (see p. 45)

  Come with *me.* This is a gift for *them.* Lord be with *you.*

- REFLEXIVE PRONOUNS—These pronouns refer back to the subject of the sentence (p. 173).

  He saw *himself* in the water. They freed *themselves* from danger.

- INTERROGATIVE PRONOUNS—These pronouns are used in questions at the beginning of the question sentence. They are the first words, unless they are objects of a preposition (see p. 161).

  *Who* is coming? *What* did the god say? *Whom* did you see? With *whom* are you living? From *whom* is the gift? In *what* is it wrapped?

- DEMONSTRATIVE PRONOUNS—These pronouns are used to point out persons or things (see p. 176).

  *This* is beautiful. *That* is ugly.
  *These* can be planted now. *Those* are ruined.

- POSSESSIVE PRONOUNS—These pronouns are used to show possession (see p. 172).

  Whose house is this? It is *mine.* *Yours* is on the next street.

- RELATIVE PRONOUNS—These pronouns are used to introduce relative subordinate clauses (see p. 179).

  The god *who* came is powerful.
  The goddess *whom* you worship is listening to your prayers.

- INDEFINITE PRONOUNS—These pronouns indicate certain people or things not clearly seen.

  *Someone* is coming. I can make out *something.* *One* should be careful.

Since the indefinite pronouns in Latin correspond in usage to their English equivalents, there is no special section devoted to this type of pronoun. The various indefinite pronouns can be studied as vocabulary entries in your textbook.

**In Latin:** There are also different types of pronouns in Latin. They are different from English pronouns in that Latin pronouns always reflect case, gender and number. This handbook and your Latin textbook will indicate to you the rules of agreement for the various types of pronouns.

## What is a Personal Pronoun?

A **PERSONAL PRONOUN** is a word taking the place of a noun which refers to a person or a thing.

> *I* am very happy.
> *They* enjoy learning Latin.
> Please look at *me*.
> The nymph liked the flower and picked *it*.

In both English and Latin, personal pronouns have different forms to show the pronoun's function in the sentence; these forms are called **CASE FORMS** (see **What is Meant by Case?**, p. 14).

A. Personal pronouns used as subject

In the following example, personal pronouns are used as subjects.

*He* ran, but *I* walked.

*Who* ran? Answer: He.
*He* is the subject of the verb *ran.*

*Who* walked? Answer: I.
*I* is the subject of the verb *walked.*

**In English:** A different personal pronoun will be used depending on the person being referred to. Here is a list of the personal pronouns used as subjects. They are said to be in the **SUBJECTIVE** or **NOMINATIVE CASE.**

| Singular | Plural | |
|---|---|---|
| I | we | the person(s) speaking; called 1st person |
| you | you | used for the person(s) spoken to; called 2nd person |
| he, she, it | they | used for the person(s) or thing(s) spoken about; called 3rd person |

As you can see, these pronouns have a different form for each person (or persons) to which they refer. Some personal pronouns also show number; that is, they show whether one person or more than one is involved. *We* and *they* are plural pronouns, *I* and *he* are singular; *you* is the same form for both singular and plural.

Let us compare the subject pronouns of English and Latin. In both languages, pronouns used as subjects are in the subjective or nominative case (see **What is Meant by Case?**, p. 14). Although the case system is much more developed in Latin than in English, understanding cases of pronouns in English can help you understand how cases work in Latin.

| English | | Latin |
|---|---|---|
| nominative (subjective) case | | nominative case |
| *I* | 1st person singular<br>the person speaking | **ego** |
| *you* | 2nd person singular<br>the person spoken to | **tū** |
| *he*<br>*she*<br>*it* | 3rd person singular<br>the person or thing<br>spoken about | **is** (masc.)<br>**ea** (fem.)<br>**id** (neut.) |
| *we* | 1st person plural<br>the person speaking<br>+ others | **nōs** |
| *you* | 2nd person plural<br>the persons spoken to | **vōs** |
| *they* | 3rd person plural<br>the persons or things<br>spoken about | **eī** (masc.)<br>**eae** (fem.)<br>**ea** (neut.) |

Let us look more closely at the two subject pronouns: *you* and *it* which have more than one Latin form so that you can learn how to choose the correct one.

*YOU*—the singular and plural form

**In English:** There is no difference between "you" in the singular and "you" in the plural. For example, if there were many people in a room and you asked aloud, "Are *you* coming with me?," the "you" could stand for one person or for many.

**In Latin:** There is a difference between "you" in the singular and "you" in the plural.

- ***You** are the cause of my grief.*

  *You* refers to one person.
  Use singular **tū.**

  **Tū** es causa dolōris meī.

• ***You** are all friends.*

*You* refers to many people.
Use plural **vōs.**

**Vōs** omnēs sunt amīcī.

*IT*—the gender of the third person pronoun

**In English:** The neuter pronoun *it* is used to replace the noun for any object or idea.

My sword is precious. *It* saved my life.
I love my country. *It* has good citizens.
Where is that temple? *It* is in the city.

**In Latin:** Since Latin nouns have gender (see **What is Meant by Gender?**, p. 7), the pronouns which replace them must show the proper gender. Thus a pronoun will be either masculine, feminine, or neuter according to the gender of the noun to which it refers.

To choose the correct form of *it* **(is, ea, id)**, you must:

1. Find the noun *it* replaces (the antecedent).
2. Determine the gender of the antecedent in Latin.
3. Determine the function of *it* in the sentence.[1]
4. Choose the case which corresponds to the function found in step. 3.

• *My sword is precious.* ***It*** *saved my life.*

Noun *it* replaces: sword **(gladius)**
Gender: **Gladius** is masculine.
Function: subject of *saved*
Case: nominative

Gladius meus est cārus. **Is** vītam meam servāvit.[2]
masc. sing.
subject = nominative

[1]Since this section is devoted to subject pronouns, *it* in all the examples is a subject. Do not forget it can also be an object (see p. 45).

[2]The subject pronouns (**is, ea, id**) could be omitted in the sample sentences if the subject were perfectly clear or were not being stressed. In these sentences the subject *is* being stressed. The context will guide you whether or not the Latin pronoun needs to be expressed.

- *I love my country. **It** has good citizens.*

    Noun *it* replaces: country (**patriam**)
    Gender: **Patriam** is feminine.
    Function: subject of *has*
    Case: nominative

  Patriam amō. **Ea** cīvēs bonōs habet.
  
  (**Ea**: fem. sing.; subject = nominative)

- *Where is that temple? **It** is in the city.*

    Noun *it* replaces: temple (**templum**)
    Gender: **Templum** is neuter.
    Function: subject of *is*
    Case: nominative

  Ubi est illud templum? **Id** est in urbe.
  
  (**Id**: neut. sing.; subject = nominative)

B. Personal pronouns as objects

In the following examples a personal pronoun is used as an object:

- He saw *us.*

    He saw *whom?* Us.
    *Us* is the direct object of *saw.*

- They wrote *me* a letter.

    They wrote *to whom?* Me.
    *Me* is the indirect object of *wrote.*

- The house is behind *you.*

  The house is *behind whom?* You.
  *You* is the object of the preposition *behind.*

**In English:** Most pronouns that occur as objects in a sentence are different from the ones used as subjects. When pronouns are used as direct or indirect objects or as objects of prepositions in English, they are said to be in the objective case (see **What are Objects?**, p. 31).

- *He* and *I* work for the farmer.

  subject = personal pronouns in the nominative case

- They invited *him* and *me.*

  direct objects = personal pronouns in the objective case

- I gave *them* my best work.

  indirect object = personal pronoun in the objective case

- They are coming with *you* and *her.*

  objects of preposition = personal pronouns in the objective case

Compare the nominative and objective cases in English for the personal pronouns:

| Nominative | Objective |
|---|---|
| I | me |
| you | you |
| he, she, it | him, her, it |
| we | us |
| you | you |
| they | them |

**In Latin:** Instead of a single objective case, there are four cases of pronouns which are used for pronoun objects: the genitive, the dative, the accusative, and the ablative. The use of these different cases corresponds to the use of the same cases of nouns. The genitive, dative, accusative, and ablative forms for the personal pronouns corresponding to the ones above are as follows:

| Nominative | | | Genitive[1] | Dative | Accusative | Ablative |
|---|---|---|---|---|---|---|
| Person | | | | Singular | | |
| 1 | | ego | meī | mihi | mē | mē |
| 2 | | tū | tuī | tibi | tē | tē |
| 3 | *m.* | is | eius | eī | eum | eō |
| | *f.* | ea | eius | eī | eam | eā |
| | *n.* | id | eius | eī | id | eō |
| | | | | Plural | | |
| 1 | | nōs | nostrī | nōbīs | nōs | nōbīs |
| 2 | | vōs | vestrī | vōbīs | vōs | vōbīs |
| 3 | *m.* | eī | eōrum | eīs | eōs | eīs |
| | *f.* | eae | eārum | eīs | eās | eīs |
| | *n.* | ea | eōrum | eīs | ea | eīs |

In general, once you have learned the functions of Latin cases of nouns, you will have no difficulty using the cases of the pronouns.

N.B.: Remember that the Latin personal pronouns in the third person replace nouns having certain genders. (This has been discussed in detail for the third person in the nominative case on p. 43). Make sure that the gender of the pronoun is the same as the gender of the noun that you are replacing.

Let us use the plural of the pronouns to give you practice in these forms.

[1]This use of the genitive is an objective use described on p. 30.

- *Are you calling the girls?* Vocāsne puellās?[1] (feminine plural) — *Yes, I am calling* ***them.*** Ita, **eās** vocō. (feminine plural accusative object)

- *Are you reading the books?* Legisne librōs? (masculine plural) — *Yes, I am reading* ***them.*** Ita, **eōs** legō. (masculine plural accusative object)

- *Are you building temples?* Aedificāsne templa? (neuter plural) — *Yes, I am building* ***them.*** Ita, **ea** aedificō. (neuter plural accusative object)

Summary: In deciding which form of a personal pronoun to use in a Latin sentence, you will need to ask yourself the following questions:

1. To which person does the pronoun refer? (1st, 2nd, 3rd, singular or plural)

    - If it is the 2nd person, be careful to distinguish between *you* singular and *you* plural.

    - If it is the 3rd person, remember to have the gender of the pronoun agree with the gender of the noun replaced.

2. How does the pronoun function in the sentence? (subject. direct object, indirect object, etc.)

    *They* live in Rome.
    (*They*: subject)

[1]When ancient Romans needed to signal that a sentence was a question they did not use our question mark. One of the ways they did so was by attaching **-ne** to the first word in the sentence.

We see *him*.
direct object

We wrote *her* a letter.
indirect object

They were writing about *us*.
object of preposition *about*

The Lord be with *you*.
object of preposition *with*

We sent you to *them*.
object of preposition *to*

3. What case in Latin is required for that particular function of the pronoun?

*They* live in Rome.
subject = nominative

We see *him*.
direct object = accusative

We wrote *her* a letter.
indirect object = dative

They were writing about *us*.
object of preposition *about* = ablative

The Lord be with *you*.
object of preposition *with* = ablative

We sent you to *them*.
object of preposition *to* = accusative

4. Select the proper form (case, gender and number) according to steps 1-3.

- ***They** live in the city.*
  **Eī** (*the men*) in urbe habitant.
  3rd person masculine plural nominative

  **Eae** (*the women*) in urbe habitant.
  3rd person feminine plural nominative

- *We see **him.***
  **Eum** vidēmus.
  3rd person masculine singular accusative

- *We wrote **her** a letter.*
  Epistulam **eī** scrīpsimus.
  3rd person feminine singular dative

- *They were writing about **us.***
  Dē **nōbīs** scribēbant.
  1st person plural ablative (object of preposition **de**)

- *The Lord be with **you.***
  Dominus **vōbīs**cum.
  2nd person plural ablative (object of preposition **cum**)

  **Cum** is often attached to its pronoun object to form a single word.

- *We sent you to **them.***
  Tē ad **eōs** mīsimus. [To the men.]
  3rd person plural accusative (object of preposition **ad**)

  Tē ad **eās** mīsimus. [To the women.]
  3rd person plural accusative (object of preposition **ad**)

## What is a Verb?

A VERB is a word that expresses an action or condition. The action can be physical, as in such verbs as *run, walk, climb, sing,* or mental as in such verbs as *dream, think, believe,* and *hope.* Verbs like *be* and *become* express a state or condition rather than an action.

The verb is one of the most important words in a sentence; you usually cannot express a complete thought without a verb.

To help you learn to recognize verbs, here is a paragraph where the verbs are in italics. Some of the verbs are single words, and some are VERB PHRASES, that is groups of words that make up a single verb idea.

The myth about Jupiter who ***came*** to earth in the form of a human being ***is*** familiar to many people. Jupiter, the king of the gods, ***decided*** *to test*[1] the hospitality of the people in a certain village. He ***had taken*** his son Mercury with him, and when the two ***had entered*** the village and ***had sought*** refuge for the night in many homes, every home ***was closed*** to them. The villagers ***stoned*** the strangers and ***set*** their dogs on them. Only the old Philemon and his wife Baucis ***welcomed*** the strangers in their humble cottage. Although they ***thought*** the strangers poor wanderers, they ***set*** their best table for the strangers. They even ***tried*** *to kill*[1] their only goose so that they ***could prepare*** a feast for the strangers. In return for such kindness the gods ***made*** the food and the wine permanent in the house and ***changed*** the humble cottage into a temple with the old couple as caretakers. They ***transformed*** the wicked villagers into fish which ***swam*** in a lake where once ***had stood*** the town. Finally, in ***granting***[2] the request that the two pious ones ***die*** at the same time, the gods ***changed*** the old Philemon and his wife Baucis into trees that ***are*** still ***standing*** on each side of the entrance to the temple.

---

[1]Infinitive (see p. 55).
[2]Verbal noun or gerund (see p. 90).

There are two kinds of verbs in both English and Latin: transitive and intransitive.

A **TRANSITIVE VERB** is a verb which takes a direct object (see **What are Objects?**, p. 31). It is indicated by the abbreviation *v.t.* (verb transitive) in the dictionary.

The old couple *welcomed* the strangers.
(*welcomed*: transitive verb; *the strangers*: direct object)

The gods *changed* the cottage into a temple.
(*changed*: transitive verb; *the cottage*: direct object)

An **INTRANSITIVE VERB** is a verb that does not take a direct object. It is indicated in the dictionary by the abbreviation *v.i.* (verb intransitive).

Philemon and Baucis *were* kind to the gods.
(*were*: intransitive verb (no direct object))

The trees still *stand* on either side of the entrance.
(*stand*: intransitive verb (no direct object))

Many verbs can be used both transitively and intransitively, depending on whether or not they have a direct object in the sentence.

The gods *entered* the house.
(*entered*: transitive verb; *the house*: direct object)

The gods *entered.*
(*entered*: intransitive verb (no direct object))

## What are the Principal Parts of a Verb?

The **PRINCIPAL PARTS** of a verb are those forms which we need to known in order to form all the different tenses.

**In English:** If we know the INFINITIVE, the PAST TENSE, and the PAST PARTICIPLE of any verb, we can apply regular rules to form all the other tenses of that verb. These three forms constitute the principal parts of an English verb.

For example, in order to form the six main tenses of the verb ***to eat***, we need to know the parts *eat* (the form used in the infinitive), *ate* (simple past), and *eaten* (past participle). The form used in the infinitive (*eat*) is also called the **DICTIONARY FORM** of the verb, since this is the way the verb is listed in the dictionary. It appears in the dictionary without the "to."

| | |
|---|---|
| Present | I eat |
| Past | I ate |
| Future | I shall eat |
| Present Perfect | I have eaten |
| Past Perfect | I had eaten |
| Future Perfect | I shall have eaten |

The principal parts of a verb are either regular or irregular.

- **REGULAR VERBS** form their past tense and their past participle very predictably with the DICTIONARY FORM OF THE VERB + *-ED*, *-D* OR *-T*.

| Infinitive[1] | Past tense | Past participle |
|---|---|---|
| to walk | walked | walked |
| to seem | seemed | seemed |
| to burn | burned or burnt | burned or burnt |

[1]The infinitive is the dictionary form of the verb preceded by the preposition *to*.

Since the past tense and the past participle of regular verbs are identical, these verbs really have only two principal parts, the infinitive and the past tense form.

- **IRREGULAR VERBS** have unpredictable principal parts. As we grow up, we learn these forms simply by hearing them, although some of them give us difficulty and require extra effort to master. Examples of verbs with irregular principal parts include the following:

| Infinitive | Past tense | Past participle |
|---|---|---|
| to sing | sang | sung |
| to draw | drew | drawn |
| to hit | hit | hit |
| to lie | lay | lain |
| to ride | rode | ridden |
| to be | was | been |

**In Latin:** There are four principal parts of a verb: the first person singular of the present tense, the infinitive, the first person singular of the perfect, followed by the perfect passive participle.

| Present tense<br>1st person singular | Infinitive | Perfect tense<br>1st person singular | Perfect passive participle |
|---|---|---|---|
| amō | amāre | amāvī | amātum |
| *I love, am loving, do love* | *to love* | *I loved, have loved, did love* | *having been loved* |

In the vocabulary of your textbook and in the dictionary, Latin verbs are listed under the first person singular of the present tense. For example, the verb *to love* is listed under **amō.** The entry gives the four principal parts listed as: **amō, -āre, -āvī, -ātum** with part of the stem or base understood to be continued for each form. (Turn to p. 61 to see how the stem or base is determined.) It is important to learn the principal parts of the verb, since the different tenses depend on the different forms. When you look up a verb in the dictionary or in the vocabulary at the back of your textbook, the principal parts will be given, and you must be able to recognize the verb in any of the forms that are based on these principal parts. Many of them follow a regular pattern. For example, the perfect of most first conjugation verbs is formed by adding **-vī** to the stem, but the perfect of other conjugation verbs is not so regular. Some irregular verbs change completely: **ferō, ferre, tulī, lātum,** *to carry, to bear,* just like *go, went, gone,* or *eat, ate, eaten* in English. These will have to be memorized individually.

The perfect passive participle always ends in **-tum** or **-sum** (**amātum** or **vīsum**) and the meaning is *having been* + the English passive past participle: *having been loved* or *having been seen.* (See **What is Meant by Active and Passive Voice?**, p. 93.) Since this form is an adjective of the first and second declensions declined like **bonus, bona, bonum** (Group A, see p. 133), it could appear as **amātus, amāta,** or the neuter **amātum,** as given in the principal parts.

## What is an Infinitive?

An **INFINITIVE** is a form of a verb without person or number.

**In English:** The infinitive is composed of two words, *TO* + VERB: *to love, to walk, to think, to enjoy, to be.* When you look up a verb in a dictionary you find it without the *to: love, walk, think, enjoy, be.* In a sentence the infinitive is always used with a conjugated verb. (See **What is a Verb Conjugation?**, p. 58.)

*To learn* is challenging.
infinitive: *To learn* — conjugated verb: is

It is important *to be* on time.
conjugated verb: is — infinitive: *to be*

Mark and Julia want *to come* home.
conjugated verb: want — infinitive: *to come*

Mark can *walk* to school.
conjugated verb: can — infinitive: *walk*

All verbs have a present infinitive and a perfect infinitive. The **PRESENT INFINITIVE** is usually *TO* + the VERB, OR just the DICTIONARY FORM OF THE VERB. The **PERFECT INFINITIVE** is *TO HAVE* + the PAST PARTICIPLE OF THE MAIN VERB.

| Present infinitive | Perfect infinitive |
|---|---|
| to be | to have been |
| to walk | to have walked |
| to think | to have thought |
| to enjoy | to have enjoyed |
| to love | to have loved |

Verbs which can be used with passive meaning (see **What is Meant by Active and Passive Voice?**, p. 93) also have present and perfect infinitive forms for the passive voice. The **PRESENT PASSIVE INFINITIVE** is formed with the verb *TO BE* + the PAST PARTICIPLE OF THE MAIN VERB, and the **PERFECT PASSIVE INFINITIVE** is formed with the phrase *TO HAVE BEEN* + the PAST PARTICIPLE OF THE MAIN VERB.

| Present passive infinitive | Perfect passive infinitive |
|---|---|
| to be loved | to have been loved |
| to be led | to have been led |

**In Latin:** The present infinitive, the second principal part of the verb,[1] ends in **-re.** It expresses in a single word the English two-word infinitive: *to sing* = **cantāre.**

It is very important to learn the infinitive form for each verb that you meet, because it gives you two essential facts:

1. The infinitive ending (the **-āre, -ēre, -ere, -īre**) enables you to identify the conjugation to which each verb belongs. The identification of a verb conjugation is fully discussed on p. 60.

2. The infinitive provides the present stem to which the endings of the present, imperfect and future tenses are attached. The verb stem is fully discussed on p. 61.

The main uses of the Latin infinitive are to complete the meaning of the conjugated verb, to function as a noun, and to be the verb in an indirect statement.

- as a complementary infinitive—to complete the meaning of another conjugated verb

*Mark and Julia want* ***to come*** *home.*

conjugated verb — *want*; infinitive — *to come*

[1]The first principal part is the first person singular, present tense, ex. **amō** (*I love*). (See **What are the Principal Parts of a Verb?**, p. 52.)

Marcus et Iūlia domum **venīre** dēsīderant.

infinitive — conjugated verb

Note the Latin word order with the infinitive before the conjugated verb.

- as a noun—especially as subject of a sentence (see p. 24)

*To learn* *is easy.*

infinitive — conjugated verb

**Discere** est facile.

infinitive — conjugated verb

- in indirect statement (see p. 120)

*He says that the gods* ***are coming.***

verb of saying — verb in a subordinate "that" clause

Dīcit deōs **venīre**.

verb of saying — infinitive in indirect statement

As in English, Latin has a present infinitive and a perfect infinitive.

| Present infinitive | | Perfect infinitive | |
|---|---|---|---|
| amāre | *to love* | amāvisse | *to have loved* |

The verbs which can be used with passive meaning have a present and a perfect infinitive form for the passive voice.

| Present passive infinitive | | Perfect passive infinitive | |
|---|---|---|---|
| amārī | *to be loved* | amātus, -a, -um esse | *to have been loved* |

Consult your textbook for details on how to form these infinitives.

Latin also has future infinitives, both active and passive. Consult your textbook for their forms, meanings and use.

## What is a Verb Conjugation?

A VERB CONJUGATION is a list of the six possible forms of the verb, one for each of the subject pronouns (1st, 2nd and 3rd persons, singular and plural). The word *conjugation* comes from two Latin words: **con** (*with*) and **jug** (*join*); the idea is that endings are joined to the stem of the verb resulting in a verb form. In Latin grammar, the word *conjugation* is also used to refer to the four main patterns of Latin verbs according to their infinitive endings.

**In English:** Verbs change very little. Let us look at the various forms of the verb ***to love*** in the present tense when each of the six possible personal pronouns is the performer of the action (see **What is a Personal Pronoun?**, p. 40).

| Person | Singular |
|---|---|
| 1st | ***I love*** the spring flowers. |
| 2nd | ***You love*** the spring flowers. |
| 3rd | ***He loves*** the spring flowers.<br>***She loves*** the spring flowers.<br>***It loves*** the spring flowers. |
| | Plural |
| 1st | ***We love*** the spring flowers. |
| 2nd | ***You love*** the spring flowers. |
| 3rd | ***They love*** the spring flowers. |

Regular verbs change very little (see *love* or *loves* above), and you do not need "to conjugate" verbs. It is simpler to say that verbs take an "-s" in the third person singular of the present tense. The irregular verb *to be* has the most forms: I *am*, you *are*, he *is*, we *are*, you *are*, they *are*.

**In Latin:** Each verb has six different endings, one for each person in the singular and in the plural. These are called PERSONAL ENDINGS.

Let us look at the same verb *to love,* **amāre**, conjugated in the present tense, to see the variety of personal endings:

| Person | Singular | Plural |
|---|---|---|
| 1st | am**ō** | amā**mus** |
| 2nd | amā**s** | amā**tis** |
| 3rd | ama**t** | ama**nt** |

Since the personal endings indicate the subject, the subject pronoun does not have to be expressed; i.e. **-ō** ending can only refer to "I." A special word must be added about the third person singular (*he/she/it*). Since **-t** may refer to a masculine, feminine or neuter subject, you must look in a previous sentence to find the subject to which the **-t** refers. This preceding passage is called the CONTEXT, and the context will tell you the subject.

**Marcus** canem portat. Canem **amat**.
***Mark** is carrying the dog. **He loves** the dog.*

**Iūlia** flōrēs portat. Flōrēs **amat**.
***Julia** is carrying flowers. **She loves** flowers.*

**Animal** flōrēs edit. Flōrēs **amat**.
***The animal** is eating the flowers. **It loves** flowers.*

Once you have learned the personal pronoun endings, you can attach them to any verb (see p. 61) in the four regular patterns called CONJUGATIONS.

**REGULAR VERBS**—There are four patterns, or groups, of verbs referred to as: the FIRST CONJUGATION, SECOND CONJUGATION, THIRD CONJUGATION, and FOURTH CONJUGATION, hereafter indicated by 1st, 2nd, 3rd, and 4th.

**IRREGULAR VERBS**—There are some common verbs which do not follow the regular pattern, especially **esse** (*to be*). You must learn this verb thoroughly since many verb tenses use the various tenses of **esse** in their formation. Consult your textbook for the conjugation of **esse** and other irregular verbs. You will have to memorize them individually.

To conjugate a verb, you must know the conjugation to which it belongs, its stem, and the personal endings. Let us see how it works:

1. The conjugation

   The vowel that precedes the **-re** of the infinitive form (see **What is an Infinitive?**, p. 55) will enable you to decide to which of the four Latin conjugations the verb belongs.

| Conjugation | Ending | Infinitive | |
|---|---|---|---|
| 1st | -**ā**re | am**āre** | *to love* |
| 2nd | -**ē**re | doc**ēre** | *to teach* |
| 3rd | -**ere**[1] | mitt**ere** | *to send* |
| 4th | -**ī**re | aud**īre** | *to hear* |

   It is especially important to distinguish between the long and short **-e-** in the infinitive of verbs for it indicates the difference between the 2nd conjugation (**docēre**) and the 3rd (**mittere**). The difference is not only in the sound of the vowel, but in the accent, since the long vowel draws the accent to it.

   docḗre     míttere

[1]There is a category of 3rd conjugation verbs called 3rd-**iō**, since a characteristic **-i-** appears in several forms: **faciō** (*I do, I make*), **faciēbam** (*I did, I made*), **faciam** (*I shall make*). The infinitive, however, ends in **-ere**.

You must memorize one sample verb for each of the six tenses (see **What is Meant by Tense?**, p. 63) of all four conjugations.

2. The stem

The infinitive provides you with the PRESENT STEM on which the present, imperfect and future tenses are formed. To find this stem, drop the infinitive ending **-re** from the infinitive form.

Here is a sample verb stem for each conjugation:

| Conjugation | Infinitive | Stem |
|---|---|---|
| 1st | amā**re** | amā- |
| 2nd | docē**re** | docē- |
| 3rd | mitte**re** | mitte- |
| 4th | audī**re** | audī- |

Consult your textbook for irregularities in the 3rd conjugation and for the stems to be used for the other tenses.

3. Personal endings

The personal endings are the same for the present, imperfect and future tenses in the active voice (see p. 000), except for the first person singular ("I"). In the imperfect and future tenses the personal endings are added to the stem + the tense sign (see p. 65 and p. 71).

Here is a list of the personal endings for the present, imperfect and future tenses for all four conjugations.

| Person | Singular | | Plural | |
|---|---|---|---|---|
| 1st | *I* | -ō or -m[1] | *we* | -mus |
| 2nd | *you* | -s | *you* | -tis |
| 3rd | *he/she/it* | -t | *they* | -nt |

[1]Your textbook will tell you which tenses use **-ō** and which use **-m** as the ending of the first person singular.

Let us look at some verbs of the first conjugation so that you can see how the pattern applies to all verbs in the same conjugation.

- all have an infinitive ending in **-āre**

  amāre *to love*   portāre *to carry*   cantāre *to sing*

- all form their stem by dropping the **-re** of the infinitive

  amā-   portā-   cantā-

- all add the same personal endings to form the present tense

| Person | | Singular | |
|---|---|---|---|
| 1st | am**ō** | port**ō** | cant**ō** |
| 2nd | amā**s** | portā**s** | cantā**s** |
| 3rd | ama**t** | porta**t** | canta**t** |
| | | Plural | |
| 1st | amā**mus** | portā**mus** | cantā**mus** |
| 2nd | amā**tis** | portā**tis** | cantā**tis** |
| 3rd | ama**nt** | porta**nt** | canta**nt** |

N.B.: The vowel before the ending is marked long in the first and second persons, but not before final **-t** and **-nt** in the third person.

Your Latin textbook lists the complete pattern for the other three conjugations, some of which have slight irregularities. There are other personal endings for the present perfect tense (see p. 66) and for the passive voice (see p. 95). The complete listings of the forms are given both in the lessons and in the back of your textbook in complete conjugations for all tenses. The complete conjugations give the pattern for a sample verb in all tenses in each conjugation and list all the irregular verbs as well.

## What is Meant by Tense?

The TENSE of a verb indicates when the action of the verb takes place: at the present time, in the past, or in the future. The word for tense comes from the Latin **tempus**, meaning *time*. Let us look at the times in the following example:

| | |
|---|---|
| I eat. | Present |
| I ate. | Past |
| I shall eat. | Future |

As you can see in the above examples, just by putting the verb in a different tense and without giving any additional information (such as "I eat *now*," or "I ate *yesterday*," or "I shall eat *tomorrow*"), you can indicate when the action of the verb takes place. There are six main tenses in English: present, past, future, present perfect, past perfect (called also pluperfect in Latin), and future perfect. Each of these tenses will be discussed separately.

## What is the Present Tense?

The PRESENT TENSE indicates that the action is going on at the present time. It can be:

- at the same time the speaker is speaking.

  I *see* you.

- an habitual action

  He *smokes* when he is nervous.

• a general truth

The sun *shines* every day.

**In English:** There are three forms of the verb which, although they have a slightly different meaning, all indicate the present tense.

| | |
|---|---|
| Pan *watches* the beautiful nymph. | Simple present |
| Pan *is watching* the beautiful nymph. | Present progressive |
| Pan *does watch* the beautiful nymph. | Present emphatic |

When a verb consists of more than one word (*is watching, does watch*), it is called a **VERB PHRASE**.

**In Latin:** There is only one verb form to indicate the present tense. It is indicated by the ending of the verb added to the stem, without any helping verb such as *is* or *does*. It is very important, therefore, not to translate these helping verbs used in English. Simply put the verb in the present tense.

Pan *watches* the beautiful nymph.
**spectat**

Pan *is watching* the beautiful nymph.
**spectat**

Pan *does watch* the beautiful nymph.
**spectat**

When you are translating a Latin verb in the present tense into English, you will have to choose the most appropriate of the three meanings according to the context.

In Latin the present tense is used, as in English, to express action now, habitual action, and general truths.

## What is the Past Tense?

The **PAST TENSE** is used to express an action that occurred previously, some time in the past.

**In English:** There are several verb forms that indicate that the action took place in the past.

| | |
|---|---|
| I worked | Simple past |
| I was working | Past progressive |
| I did work | Past emphatic |

The simple past, consisting of only one word, refers to a completed act. The past progressive (a continuing act) and the past emphatic (with a fist banging on the table for emphasis), consisting of more than one word, are **COMPOUND TENSES** or **VERB PHRASES.**

English has three other compound tenses for expressing past actions. These are the perfect tenses, and they consist of more than one word. They are therefore verb phrases.

| | |
|---|---|
| I have worked | Present perfect |
| I had worked | Past perfect |
| I shall have worked | Future perfect |

These last three tenses will be discussed in separate sections.

**In Latin:** Two verb tenses indicating past time deserve particular attention: the **IMPERFECT** and the **PERFECT** (called *present perfect* in English).

- The imperfect is formed with the PRESENT STEM + THE IMPERFECT TENSE SIGN -*BA*- + THE PERSONAL ENDINGS: **amābam**[1] (*I loved, was loving, did love*), **amābat** (*he loved, was loving, did love*). Consult your Latin textbook for the complete pattern.

---

[1]Note that the 1st person singular ending is **-m** instead of **-ō** (see p. 61).

- The perfect tense is based on the third principal part of the verb (see **What are the Principal Parts of a Verb?**, p. 52) which provides the PERFECT STEM.

  Principal parts: amō, amāre, **amāvī**, amātum
  perfect

  To find the perfect stem drop the final **-ī** of the third principal part.

  Perfect stem: amāvī ⟶ amāv-

  The perfect tense is formed with the PERFECT STEM + THE PERFECT PERSONAL ENDINGS.

  Perfect personal endings:

| Person | Singular | | Plural | |
|---|---|---|---|---|
| 1st | *I* | -ī | *we* | -imus |
| 2nd | *you* | -istī | *you* | -istis |
| 3rd | *he/she/it* | -it | *they* | -ērunt |

  These perfect endings added on to the perfect stem form the perfect tense: **amāvit** (*he loved, did love, has loved*), **amāvērunt** (*they loved, did love, have loved*).

  All of the perfect tenses (see **What is the Past Perfect (Pluperfect) Tense?,** p. 69 and **What is the Future Perfect Tense?**, p. 73) use the perfect stem based on the third principal part, but only the perfect tense uses the perfect personal endings above.

You might encounter difficulties when you have to decide whether to use the imperfect or the perfect tense. The English verb form will rarely tell you which one of the two to select.

The imperfect and the perfect both take place in the past time. However, when the duration of one action is compared to the duration of another action in the same sentence or story, the imperfect is used for the longer or more continuous of the two actions.

I ***was reading*** when he *came* in.
imperfect — perfect

Both actions are taking place at the same time, but the action of *reading* is continuous while the *coming in* took only a few moments.

*Callisto **was walking** through the woods when suddenly she **saw** a bear.*
Callistō per silvās **ambulābat** cum subitō ursam **vīdit.**

ambulābat: continuous action = imperfect
vīdit: quickly done, once done = perfect

You might also note that there are several English expressions that indicate when the imperfect should be used:

- if the English verb form includes the idea of the helping verb *used to*

    *Narcissus **used to watch** his reflection in a pool.*
    Narcissus in stagnō imāginem suam **spectābat**.

    *As a little boy, **I obeyed** my parents.*
    Ego, puer, parentibus **parēbam**.

- if the English verb form is in the past progressive: *was laughing, was running*

    *The nymphs **were watching** the stag in the woods.*
    Nymphae cervum in silvīs **spectābant**.

- if the English verb expresses the time of a narrative in the past

    *Once there **was** a beautiful queen who **lived** in a palace.*
    Ōlim **erat** rēgīna pulchra quae in rēgiā **habitābat**.

Read through the following paragraph in English and identify which tense of the verb (imperfect or perfect) you would use for each situation in Latin. We will add the appropriate Latin verb after you have made your decision, and you can check yourself:

I *was sitting*[1] at home in the evening watching television. The dog *was sleeping*[2] beside me, and I *was*[3] not afraid because he *was*[4] a good watch dog. My husband *was working*[5] late, and my son *was sleeping*[6] upstairs. Suddenly I *heard*[7] a noise in the kitchen. The dog *sat up*[8] and *barked.*[9] I *ran*[10] upstairs and *called*[11] the police on the phone. They *arrived*[12] in minutes and *found*[13] that a broom *had fallen*[14] out of the closet.

---

[1-6] Imperfect: (1) sedēbam (2) dormiēbat (3) eram (4) erat (5) labōrābat (6) dormiēbat.
[7-13] Perfect: (7) audīvī (8) surrēxit (9) latrāvit (10) cucurrī (11) vocāvī (12) advēnērunt (13) invēnērunt.
[14] Past perfect: ceciderat (see p. 69).

## What is the Past Perfect (Pluperfect) Tense?

The **PAST PERFECT TENSE** is used to express an action completed in the past before some other past action or event.

**In English:** It is formed with the auxiliary *HAD*+ THE PAST PARTICIPLE OF THE MAIN VERB: *had eaten, had taken.* The past perfect is used when two actions happened at different times in the past, and you want to make it clear which of the actions preceded the other.

She suddenly *remembered* that she *had* not *eaten.*

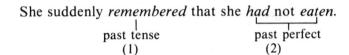

past tense (1) — past perfect (2)

Both action (1) and action (2) occurred in the past, but action (2) preceded action (1). Therefore, action (2) is in the past perfect.

Do not forget that verb tenses indicate the time that an action occurred. Therefore, when verbs in the same sentence are in the imperfect, the action took place at the same time.

Niobe *was weeping* because Apollo *was killing* her sons.

past progressive (1) — past progressive (2)

Action (1) and action (2) took place at the same time.

In order to show that the actions took place at different times, a different tense must be used.

Niobe *was weeping* because Apollo *had killed* her sons.

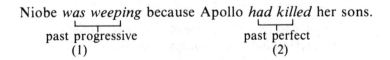

past progressive (1) — past perfect (2)

Action (2) took place before action (1).

**In Latin:** The Latin term for past perfect is PLUPERFECT. The pluperfect tense is formed with the PERFECT STEM + THE IMPERFECT FORMS OF *ESSE* to form a single word: **cantāv** + **-eram, -erās, -erat, -erāmus, -erātis, -erant**; **cantāv** + **-erat** → **cantāverat** (*he had sung*).

The pluperfect is used to make clear that an action took place before another action in the past. Study the relationship of tenses in this time line and how they are applied to the English and Latin examples in this section.

| Verb tense: | **Pluperfect** | **Perfect**<br>**Imperfect** | **Present** | **Future** |
|---|---|---|---|---|
| | D | C | B | A |
| Time action | X | X | X | X |
| takes place: | before "C" | before "B" | now | tomorrow or beyond sometime after "B" |

In Latin and in English the same relationship exists between the tense of the verb and the time when the action takes place.

- same verb tense = same time

  *Niobe* ***was weeping*** *because Apollo* ***was killing*** *her sons.*
  Niobē **lacrimābat** quia Apollo fīliōs **necābat**.
  imperfect "C" — imperfect "C"

- different verb tenses = different times

  *Niobe* ***was weeping*** *because Apollo* ***had killed*** *her sons.*
  Niobē **lacrimābat** quia Apollo fīliōs **necāverat**.
  imperfect "C" — pluperfect "D"

## What is the Future Tense?

The FUTURE TENSE is used to describe an action which will take place in time to come, the future.

**In English:** It is formed by means of the auxiliary verb *WILL* OR *SHALL* + DICTIONARY FORM OF THE MAIN VERB.

> Thisbe *will arrive* first.
> Pyramus *will grieve* for her death.
> We *shall listen* to the story.[1]

English often uses the auxiliary *shall* for the first person singular and plural and *will* for the second and third persons to express the future: *I shall listen; you and he will listen.*

In conversation, *shall* and *will* are often shortened to *'ll*: You*'ll do* it tomorrow; I*'ll listen* to the music.

**In Latin:** You do not need an auxiliary verb to show that the action will take place in the future. Instead the tense signs **-bi-** and **-e-** are used between the stem and the personal endings. The future tense is formed with the PRESENT STEM + *-BI-* (for 1st and 2nd conjugations) OR *-E-* (for 3rd and 4th conjugations) + THE PERSONAL ENDINGS: **cantābit** (*he/she/it will sing*), **docēbimus** (*we shall teach*), **mittēs** (*you will send*), **audient** (*they will hear*).

The tense signs (**-bi-** and **-e-**) signal future time, but there are irregularities. Study the sample verbs given in the conjugations in your Latin textbook.

The use of the future in Latin corresponds to its use in English.

---

[1]These sentences are based on the sad tale of Pyramus and Thisbe, young lovers whose marriage is prevented by their parents. They agree to meet secretly and through mistakes kill themselves thinking each has caused the other's death.

Thisbē prīma **adveniet**.
future

*Thisbe **will arrive** first.*

Pȳramus mortem eius **dolēbit**.
future

*Pyramus **will grieve for** her death.*

Latin is much stricter than English in its use of tenses. While English occasionally uses the present tense for an action that will take place in the future, Latin uses the future tense. For example, English uses the present after *when*, while Latin uses the future.

*Pyramus will grieve when he **sees** Thisbe's scarf.*
future present (with future implied)

Pȳramus dolēbit cum velāmina Thisbēs **vidēbit**.
future future

## What is the Future Perfect Tense?

The FUTURE PERFECT tense is used to express an action which will be completed in the future prior to another future action.

**In English:** The future perfect is formed with the auxiliaries *WILL HAVE* OR *SHALL HAVE* + THE PAST PARTICIPLE OF THE MAIN VERB: *I shall have taken, he will have eaten.*

You will often find the future perfect used for the verb in the main clause (see **What are Sentences, Phrases and Clauses?**, p. 108), after a subordinate clause introduced by "when" or "by the time." The verb of the subordinate clause is in the present tense but a future time is implied.

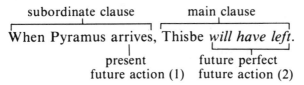

subordinate clause — main clause

When Pyramus arrives, Thisbe *will have left*.

arrives: present, future action (1)
*will have left*: future perfect, future action (2)

Both action (1) and (2) will occur at some future time, but action (2) will be completed before action (1) takes place. Therefore, action (2) is in the future perfect tense.

When Thisbe returns, Pyramus *will have killed* himself.

returns: present implying future, future action (1)
*will have killed*: future perfect, future action (2)

Both action (1) and (2) will occur at some future time, but action (2) will be completed before action (1) takes place. Therefore action (2) is in the future perfect tense.

**In Latin:** The future perfect is formed with the PERFECT STEM + THE FUTURE FORMS OF *ESSE* to form a single word: **cantāv** + **-erō, -eris, -erit, -erimus, -eritis, -erint**; **cantāv** + **-erit** → **cantāverit** (*he will have sung*).

When you observe the following line showing the relationship of future tenses, you will see that the future perfect is used in the same way in both languages, but that the future (point "C") is expressed by the present in English and by the future in Latin (see p. 72).

| | | | |
|---|---|---|---|
| Verb tense: | **Present** A | **Future Perfect** B | **Present** (English) **Future** (Latin) C |
| Time action | X | X | X |
| takes place: | now | after "A" and before "C" | after "B" |

In the following examples, notice that actions taking place at point "B" are in the future perfect tense in both languages.

- *When Pyramus arrives, Thisbe* ***will have left.***

  present point "C" (*arrives*) — future perfect point "B" (*will have left*)

  Cum Pȳramus adveniet, Thisbē **discesserit**.

  future (*adveniet*) — future perfect (*discesserit*)

- *When Thisbe returns, Pyramus* ***will have killed*** *himself.*

  present point "C" (*returns*) — future perfect point "B" (*will have killed*)

  Cum Thisbē reveniet, Pȳramus sē **necāverit**.

  future (*reveniet*) — future perfect (*necāverit*)

Latin also uses the future perfect to express future conditions (see **What are Conditional Sentences?**, p. 126).

## What is an Auxiliary Verb?

A verb that works with another verb to make a verb phrase is called an AUXILIARY VERB or a HELPING VERB.

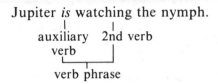

Jupiter *is* watching the nymph.

auxiliary verb — 2nd verb

verb phrase

Latona *has* seen her children die.

auxiliary verb — 2nd verb

verb phrase

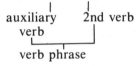

The soldiers *did* cross the river.

auxiliary verb — 2nd verb

verb phrase

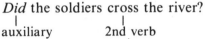

*Did* the soldiers cross the river?

auxiliary verb — 2nd verb

verb phrase

**In English:** Auxiliary verbs are often needed to express verb tenses and other sentence structures. The most common auxiliary verbs and their uses are the following:

*TO BE* (am, is, are, was, were)

- to help formulate the progressive forms of the present and past tenses (see **What is the Present Tense?**, p. 63 and **What is the Past Tense?**, p. 65)

Jupiter *is watching* the nymph.
present progressive

Apollo *was chasing* Daphne
past progressive

- to indicate the passive voice (see **What is Meant by Active and Passive Voice?**, p. 93)

The book *is read* by many students.
present passive

The play *was performed* by experienced actors.
past passive

*TO DO* (do, does, did)

- to help formulate the emphatic forms of the present and past tenses (see **What is the Present Tense?**, p. 63 and **What is the Past Tense?**, p. 65)

Jupiter *does like* to watch the nymphs.
present emphatic

Pan *did make* a flute out of reeds.
past emphatic

- to help formulate questions

*Does* Jupiter *watch* the nymph?
verb phrase in a question

*Did* Apollo *chase* Daphne?
verb phrase in a question

*TO HAVE* (has, have, had)

- to help formulate the perfect tenses (see **What is the Past Tense?**, p. 65; **What is the Past Perfect (Pluperfect) Tense?**, p. 69; and **What is the Future Perfect Tense?**, p. 73)

Latona *has called* her children.
perfect

Pan *had breathed* over the reeds.
past perfect

*WILL* and *SHALL*

- to indicate the future tense (see **What is the Future Tense?**, p. 71)

Apollo *will kill* the sons of Niobe.
future

*Shall* we *go* to the city together?
future

N.B.: The verbs *to be, to do* and *to have* can also be used as main verbs, that is, used alone without "helping" another verb.

- Jupiter *is* a god.
main verb

Jupiter *is watching* the nymph.
auxiliary verb
verb phrase

- The soldiers *did* an evil deed.
main verb

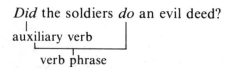

*Did* the soldiers *do* an evil deed?

auxiliary verb

verb phrase

- Latona *has* two children.

main verb

Latona *has called* her children.

auxiliary verb

verb phrase

English has some auxiliary verbs which express shades or moods of meaning. For that reason the verbs are sometimes called **MODAL** (mood) **AUXILIARIES**. These verbs, such as *can, could, may, might, should, would, must,* etc., show that the action expressed by the verb phrase is not actually occurring, but possibly can or may or ought to happen.

Atalanta *can win* the race easily.
Hippomenes *may win* the race.
If he *should lose*, he *must die*.

**In Latin:** The idea that is expressed by a verb phrase in English is usually expressed by a single verb in Latin.

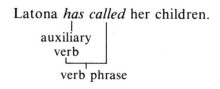

Jupiter ***is watching*** the nymph.

present progressive

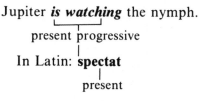

In Latin: **spectat**

present

Latona ***has called*** her children.

present perfect

In Latin: **vocāvit**

perfect

The book ***is read*** by many students.

present passive

In Latin: **legitur**

present passive

Jupiter ***does like*** to watch the nymphs.

present emphatic

In Latin: **amat**

present

***Did*** the soldiers ***cross*** the river?

to formulate question (past)

In Latin: **trānsiēruntne**

perfect + **ne**[1]

Apollo ***will kill*** the sons of Niobe.

to formulate future

In Latin: **necābit**

future

[1]**Ne** asks a question (see p. 118).

## What is a Participle?

A **PARTICIPLE** is a verb form which is part verb and part adjective; it is called a **VERBAL ADJECTIVE**. In English, there are two participles: the present participle and the past participle. In Latin, there are also the future participles.

A. The present participle

**In English:** The present participle is easy to recognize because it is the ***-ing*** form of the verb: *running, working, studying.*

The present participle has two functions:

1. as part of a verb phrase to form the progressive forms (see p. 76)

Theseus is *entering* the labyrinth.[1]
verb phrase

Ariadne was *trying* to help Theseus.
verb phrase

2. as an adjective to describe a noun or pronoun

- a descriptive attributive adjective (see p. 132)

Theseus was an *outstanding* hero.
describes the noun *hero*

- a predicate adjective (see p. 132)

Theseus was *outstanding*.
refers back to the subject *Theseus*

---

[1]Theseus, aided by the princess Ariadne who gave him a ball of string, entered the maze called the Labyrinth and killed the Minotaur, a creature half-man and half-bull.

- an adjective introducing a participial phrase (see p. 110)

Theseus, *seeing* the Minotaur, was not afraid.

The entire phrase *seeing the Minotaur* works as an adjective modifying *Theseus.*

No one saw Theseus *killing* the Minotaur.

The entire phrase *killing the Minotaur* works as an adjective modifying *Theseus.*

**In Latin:** The present participle is called the PRESENT ACTIVE PARTICIPLE, since it is always active in meaning (see **What is Meant by Active and Passive Voice?**, p. 93). It too is part verb and part adjective. It is formed with the PRESENT STEM OF THE VERB + *-NS* (nom. sing.), *-NTIS* (gen. sing.) and is an adjective of the third declension (Group B, see p. 134), declined in all cases, singular and plural: **cantāns, cantantis** (*singing*), **docēns, docentis** (*teaching*), **mittēns, mittentis** (*sending*), **audiēns, audientis** (*hearing*). Like all adjectives in Latin, it must agree in case, gender and number with the noun or pronoun it modifies.

1. What is the case of the noun or pronoun it modifies?

2. What is the gender and number of the noun or pronoun it modifies?

The present active participle is used as an adjective to describe a noun or pronoun, or to introduce a participial phrase.

- a descriptive attributive adjective

*Theseus was an* ***outstanding*** *hero.*

Case: *Hero* is predicate word = nominative
Gender & Number: **Hērōs** is masculine singular.

Thēseus erat hēros **praestāns.**

present active participle
nominative masculine singular

*Theseus saw the* ***burning*** *palace.*

Case: *Palace* is direct object = accusative
Gender & Number: **Rēgia** (*palace*) is feminine singular.

Thēseus rēgiam **conflagrantem** vīdit.

present active participle
accusative feminine singular

- a predicate adjective

This use of the present active participle is rare. It is only used when the participle functions completely as an adjective.

Thēseus est **sapiēns**.
*Theseus is* ***wise****.* (a wise man)[1]

- an adjective introducing a participial phrase

*Theseus,* ***seeing*** *the Minotaur, was not afraid.*

Case: *Theseus* is subject = nominative
Gender & Number: **Thēseus** is masculine singular.

Thēseus Mīnōtaurum **vidēns** nōn timēbat.

present active participle
nominative masculine singular

*No one saw Theseus* ***killing*** *the Minotaur.*

Case: *Theseus* is direct object = accusative
Gender & Number: **Thēseus** is masculine singular.

Nēmo Thēseum Mīnōtaurum **necantem** vīdit.

present active participle
accusative masculine singular

---

[1]Sometimes the present participle, acting as a substantive (an adjective which has become a noun), has the meaning of a noun. **Sapiēns** can mean *wise* or a *wise man*.

As a student beginning the study of Latin, there are two things to watch out for with regard to present participles.

1. You must keep in mind that the English tenses formed with an auxiliary + present participle (*she is studying, they were dancing*) are not expressed by participles in Latin. The verb phrase in English corresponds to a Latin tense.

   - *Orpheus* ***is singing***.[1]
     present progressive

     Orpheus **cantat**.
     present

   - *The animals* ***were listening***.
     past progressive

     Animālia **audiēbant**.
     imperfect

   - *Eurydice* ***will be coming***.
     future progressive

     Eurydicē **veniet**.
     future

   The tense of the auxiliary verb in English corresponds to the tense of the Latin verb. Consult the sections on tenses of verbs.

[1]The wedding of the famous singer Orpheus was spoiled when the bride, Eurydice, was bitten by a snake and died. She went to the Underworld, but Orpheus, who could move even animals and rocks with his music, persuaded the king and queen of that region to allow Eurydice to return to Earth. He was not allowed to look back at her, but unfortunately he could not resist a backward glance. She disappeared a second time, this time forever.

2. What might appear to be a present participle (a verbal adjective) because it is a verb form ending in *-ing* could be a gerund (a verbal noun). Be sure to consult the section **What is a Verbal Noun (a Gerund)?**, p. 90. Included there is a chart summarizing the various English *-ing* forms and their Latin equivalents on p. 92.

B. The past participle

**In English:** The past participle is the verb form used following "I have": *I have taken, I have helped, I have written.*

The "regular" verbs form their past participle with the DICTIONARY FORM OF THE VERB + *-ED, -D* OR *-T.*

| Dictionary form | Past participle |
|---|---|
| help | help*ed* |
| hear | hear*d* |
| walk | walk*ed* |
| burn | burn*ed* or burn*t* |

The irregular verbs form their past participle in no set manner, and each must be learned separately.

| Dictionary form | Past participle |
|---|---|
| eat | eaten |
| teach | taught |
| write | written |
| sing | sung |

The past participle has two functions:

1. as part of a verb phrase

- active (see p. 77)

The mighty city of Troy has *fallen*.[1]
verb phrase

Many Trojan heroes have *died*.
verb phrase

Helen hadn't (had not) *seen* her husband for many years.
verb phrase

- passive (see p. 94)

Many Trojan heroes were *killed* in the war.
verb phrase

The Trojan horse was *dragged* into the city.
verb phrase

2. as an adjective to describe a noun or pronoun

- a descriptive attributive adjective

The *captured* city was burned by the Greeks.
describes the noun *city*

Hecuba buried her *murdered* sons.
describes the noun *sons*

**In Latin:** The past participle is called the **PERFECT PASSIVE PARTICIPLE**, since it is normally passive in meaning. The past participle must be learned with each verb as the fourth principal part (see

[1]The Trojan War was fought by the Greeks to recover the beautiful Queen Helen, who had been abducted by the Trojan Paris, son of Priam, king of Troy. The Greeks finally destroyed the city of Troy, having entered it through the ruse of a Wooden Horse. They murdered Priam, his sons, and most of the Trojans, but took the Queen Hecuba as a captive. Helen was returned to her husband.

**What are the Principal Parts of a Verb?**, p. 52) ending in **-tum** or **-sum.**[1] It is an adjective of the first and second declension declined like **bonus, -a, -um** (Group A, see p. 133): **cantātum** (*having been sung*), **doctum** (*having been taught*), **missum** (*having been sent*), **audītum** (*having been heard*). Like all adjectives in Latin, it must agree in case, gender and number with the noun or pronoun it modifies.

The perfect passive participle has two major functions:

1. as a part of a verb phrase to form perfect tenses of the passive voice

*The city of Troy was **burned** by the Greeks.*

Case: *City* is subject = nominative
Gender & Number: **Urbs** (*city*) is feminine singular.

Urbs Trōia a Graecīs **incensa** est.

perfect passive participle (fem. sing.) + **est**

2. as an adjective modifying a noun

- a descriptive attributive adjective

*The Greeks burned the **captured** city.*

Case: *City* is direct object = accusative
Gender & Number: **Urbem** (*city*) is feminine singular.

Graecī urbem **captam** incendērunt.

perfect passive participle
accusative feminine singular

*Hecuba buried her **murdered** sons.*

Case: *Sons* is direct object = accusative
Gender & Number: **Fīliōs** (*sons*) is masculine plural.

---

[1]The fourth principal part of the verb is usually given in the neuter or **-um** form. This form is called the SUPINE in some textbooks.

Hecuba fīliōs **necātōs** sepelīvit.

perfect passive participle
accusative masculine plural

- as an adjective in a participial phrase

a. introducing the participial phrase

participial phrase

***Driven** by the wind,* *the Greek ships came to Troy.*

Case: *Ships* is subject = nominative
Gender & Number: **Nāvēs** (*ships*) is feminine plural.

**Pulsae** ventō nāvēs Graecae Trōiam advēnērunt.

perfect passive participle
nominative feminine plural

participial phrase

*The Trojans saw the horse* ***left behind*** *by the Greeks.*

Case: *Horse* is direct object = accusative
Gender & Number: **Equum** (*horse*) is masculine singular.

Troiānī equum ā Graecīs **relictum** vīdērunt.

perfect passive participle
accusative masculine singular

b. within an ablative absolute

This ABLATIVE ABSOLUTE construction is very common in Latin: it consists of two words in the ablative case, most often a noun and a participle. Although it is grammatically independent (and therefore "absolute") of the subject or the object of the main clause (see p. 111), it is logically connected to explain the circumstances surrounding the action of the main verb.

ablative absolute

Mīnōtaurō **necātō**, Thēseus ab īnsulā discessit.

perfect passive participle
modifying **Mīnōtaurō**
both in ablative masculine singular

*The Minotaur **having been killed**, Theseus left the island.*

or in better English

*After the Minotaur was killed, Theseus left the island.*

Consult your textbook for a complete discussion of the ablative absolute.

Keep in mind that the equivalent of English active tenses formed with the auxiliary verb *have* + past participle (*have seen*) do not use participles in Latin. The English verb phrase corresponds to a Latin tense:

*I **have seen** the beautiful city of Troy.*

verb phrase

Urbem Trōiam pulchram **vīdī**.

perfect tense

C. The future participles

**In English:** There are no future participles.

**In Latin:** There are two future participles, active and passive (see p. 93). They are verbal adjectives, verb forms used as adjectives. We shall consider them separately since each has unique uses which must be carefully distinguished.

- The FUTURE ACTIVE PARTICIPLE is used to express an action about to be performed and corresponds to the English expression "about to" + the present form of the verb. It is formed with the stem of the perfect passive participle (4th principal part of the verb) + **-ūrus, -ūra, -ūrum.** It is an adjective of the first and second declension, declined like **bonus, -a, -um** (Group A, p. 133): **ventūrus, -a, -um,** (*about to come*), **futūrus, -a, -um** (*about to be*). Since it is an adjective, it must agree in case, gender and number with the noun it modifies.

*The gladiators **about to die** saluted the emperor.*
Gladiātōrēs **moritūrī** imperatōrem salutāvērunt.

future active participle
nom. masc. pl. modifying **gladiātōrēs**

The future active participle is often used with a form of **esse** to express an imminent action, an action about to take place. This usage is called the ACTIVE PERIPHRASTIC, from the word *periphrasis* meaning speaking in a round-about manner. It is a round-about way of expressing future time.

The Sirens ***are about to sing.***
Sirēnēs **cantātūrae sunt.**[1]

active periphrastic
fut. act. part. + **sunt**

• The FUTURE PASSIVE PARTICIPLE is commonly called the GERUNDIVE. It is formed from the PRESENT STEM + *-NDUS, -NDA, -NDUM.* It is an adjective of the first and second declension declined like **bonus, -a, -um** (Group A, p. 133): **cantandus, -a, -um** (*about to be sung*); **legendus, -a, -um** (*about to be read*). Since it is an adjective, it must agree with the noun it modifies in case, gender and number.

Librum **legendum** habeō.

future passive participle (gerundive)
acc. masc. sing. modifying **librum**

*I have a book **to be read*** (which ought to be read, must be read).

---

[1]Compare the regular future **cantābunt**, *they will sing.*

Although it literally means "about to be" + the past participle, it is not so much the fact that the act will take place in the future that is being expressed, but rather the idea of obligation or necessity to perform the act.

The future passive participle (the gerundive) is often used with a form of **esse** as a verb phrase expressing obligation or necessity. This usage is called the **PASSIVE PERIPHRASTIC**.

Hic liber **legendus est**.

passive periphrastic
fut. pass. part. (gerundive) + **est**

*This book **must be read**.*

## What is a Verbal Noun (a Gerund)?

A **GERUND** is a verb form which is part verb and part noun; it is called a **VERBAL NOUN**.

**In English:** The verbal noun, the gerund, is formed with the DICTIONARY FORM OF THE VERB + *-ING*. It can function in a sentence in almost any way that a noun can: as a subject, object of a verb or of a preposition.

*Singing* is an art.

noun from the verb *to sing*
subject of the sentence

Do you enjoy *singing*?

noun from the verb *to sing*
direct object of verb *to enjoy*

The art of *singing* is difficult.

noun from the verb *to sing*
object of the preposition *of*

Since the English *-ing* form of the verb can be part of a verb phrase, a verbal adjective (present participle), or a verbal noun (gerund), it is important to distinguish between these three uses in order to choose the correct Latin equivalent.

Maria is *singing*.

verb phrase
present tense

He was a *singing* musician.

verbal adjective
present participle

*Singing* is an art.

verbal noun
gerund

See chart on p. 92.

**In Latin:** As in English, the verbal noun can function in any way that a noun can function, except as subject or direct object of the sentence. When the verbal noun is the subject of the sentence or the direct object of the verb, Latin uses the infinitive of the verb.

- **Cantāre** est ars.

  infinitive

  ***Singing*** *is an art.*

  subject

- Amāsne **cantāre**?
  (infinitive)

  *Do you like **singing**?*
  (direct object)

It is important to distinguish between the English *-ing* form in a verb phrase (see p. 83), as a present participle (see p. 81) and as a gerund (see below). For reference, here is a chart summarizing the various English *-ing* forms and their Latin equivalents.

| English *-ing* | → | Latin equivalent |
|---|---|---|
| Verb phrase | | |
| auxiliary + present participle | → | various tenses: |
| ex. is *singing* | | present |
| was *singing* | | past |
| will be *singing* | | future |
| etc. | | etc. |
| Adjective | | |
| present participle | → | present active participle |
| ex. *singing* musician | | present stem + **-ns, -ntis** |
| Noun (gerund) | | |
| subject of sentence | → | infinitive |
| ex. *Singing* is an art. | | |
| direct object of sentence | → | infinitive |
| ex. Do you like *singing*? | | |
| other functions | → | gerund<br>present stem + **-ndī, -ndum, -ndō** |

The gerund is a neuter noun of the second declension formed from the PRESENT STEM OF THE VERB + *-NDĪ* (gen.), *-NDŌ* (dat.), *-NDUM* (acc.), *-NDŌ* (abl.). It does not exist in the nominative, since an infinitive is used for the subject in Latin. In the accusative, the gerund is used only as object of a preposition, while the infinitive is used as the direct object of a verb.

- Ars **cantandī** difficilis est.
  genitive of gerund

  *The art **of singing** is difficult.*
  object of preposition *of*

- Amāre discit **amandō**.
  ablative of gerund

  *He learns to love **by loving**.*
  object of preposition *by*

## What is Meant by Active and Passive Voice?

The voice of the verb refers to the relationship between the verb and its subject. There are two voices:

The **ACTIVE VOICE**—A sentence is said to be in the active voice when the verb expresses what the subject of the verb is or does. In this instance, the verb is called an **ACTIVE VERB**.

The king touches the food.[1]
subject — verb — direct object

[1]King Midas asked for and received the golden touch as a favor from a god. The gift seemed a blessing at first when everything turned to gold, but it became a curse when the king tried to eat and drink.

The subject, *the king,* peforms the action of the verb, *touches,* and the direct object, *the food,* is the receiver of the action.

The PASSIVE VOICE—A sentence is said to be in the passive voice when the verb expresses what is done to the subject by someone or something. In this instance the verb is called a PASSIVE VERB.

> The food is touched by the king.
> subject verb agent

The subject, *the food,* is not the performer of the action of the verb, *is touched,* but is having the action performed upon it. The doer of the action, *the king,* is called the AGENT.

**In English:** The passive voice is expressed by the verb *TO BE* conjugated in the proper tense + THE PAST PARTICIPLE OF THE MAIN VERB.

> The food *is touched* by the king.
> subject verb agent

> The race *was won* by the man.
> subject verb agent

> The nymph *had been chased* by the god.
> subject verb agent

Note that the tense of the sentence is indicated by the tense of the auxiliary verb *to be.*

> The food *is* touched by the king.
> present passive

> The food *was* touched by the king.
> past passive

The food *will be* touched by the king.

future passive

**In Latin:** Unlike English, not all passive verbs are expressed with an auxiliary verb. For the **PRESENT, IMPERFECT** and **FUTURE TENSES**, the passive voice is formed with the PRESENT STEM + THE TENSE SIGN (for the imperfect and future) + a SPECIAL SET OF PASSIVE ENDINGS. For the **PERFECT TENSES**, the passive voice is expressed by the PERFECT PASSIVE PARTICIPLE + A FORM OF *ESSE* written as two separate words forming a verb phrase.

Present, Imperfect and Future Passive

The same passive endings are used for the present, imperfect and future tenses:

| Person | Singular | | Plural | |
|---|---|---|---|---|
| 1st | *I* | -r | *we* | -mur |
| 2nd | *you* | -ris | *you* | -minī |
| 3rd | *he/she/it* | -tur | *they* | -ntur |

Present: PRESENT STEM + PASSIVE ENDINGS

Cibus ā rēge **tangitur**.

present passive

*The food* ***is touched*** *by the king.*

present

Imperfect: PRESENT STEM + *-BA-* + PASSIVE ENDINGS

Cibus ā rēge **tangēbātur**.

imperfect passive

*The food* ***was touched*** *by the king.*

past

Future: PRESENT STEM + *-BI-* OR *-E-* + PASSIVE ENDINGS

Cibus ā rēge **tangētur**.
future passive

*The food* ***will be touched*** *by the king.*
future

The passive endings are easily distinguished from the active endings.

| Active | → | Passive |
|---|---|---|
| Rēx cibum **tangit**. | | Cibus ā rēge **tangitur**. |
| S DO V (present active) | | S A V (present passive) |
| *The king* ***touches*** *the food.* | | *The food* ***is touched*** *by the king.* |

Perfect tenses in the passive

These tenses (perfect, past perfect and future perfect) require the use of an auxiliary verb. The PERFECT PASSIVE PARTICIPLE + A FORM OF *ESSE* CONJUGATED IN THE APPROPRIATE TENSES form a verb phrase.

Cibus **tactus est**.
perfect

*The food* ***has been touched.***

Cibus **tactus erat**.
past perfect (pluperfect)

*The food* ***had been touched.***

Cibus **tactus erit**.
future perfect

*The food* ***will have been touched.***

Remember that the perfect passive participles used above in verb phrases are adjectives. Therefore, they must agree with the nouns they modify (always nominative subjects) in case, gender and number.

Cibus tactus (est, erat, erit)
nominative
masculine singular (**cibus**, food, is masculine)

The agent in a passive sentence is expressed

- by the preposition **ā** (**ab** before a vowel) + the ablative when the agent is a person

  **ā** rēge      ***by** the king*

- by the ablative without a preposition when the agent is a thing

  ventō      *by the wind*

  This is called the ABLATIVE OF MEANS.

There is a type of verb particular to Latin which you must learn to recognize. These verbs have mostly passive forms, i.e. they are conjugated like passive verbs, but they have active meanings. They are called DEPONENT VERBS from the Latin verb **dēpōnere**, *to lay aside,* because they have *laid aside* their passive meaning. English does not have deponent verbs. When you learn these verbs be sure to remember that their meaning is active, although their form is passive.

Here is an example of the deponent verb **loquor, loquī, locūtus sum**[1] conjugated in the third person singular. It is translated actively. This conjugation of all tenses in a single person and number is called a SYNOPSIS, a convenient way to review all the tenses.

[1]There are only three principal parts for a deponent verb: first person singular, present tense; infinitive; first person singular, perfect tense, which includes the participle.

| | | |
|---|---|---|
| Present | loquitur | *he speaks, is speaking, does speak* |
| Imperfect | loquēbātur | *he spoke, was speaking, did speak* |
| Future | loquētur | *he will speak* |
| Perfect | locūtus est | *he has spoken, spoke, did speak* |
| Pluperfect | locūtus erat | *he had spoken* |
| Future perfect | locūtus erit | *he will have spoken* |

Note the difference in ending between the verbs **dicere**, an active verb, and **loquitur**, a deponent verb, both relating to speech.

**Dīcit** mē esse amīcum.
***He says*** *that I am his friend.*

**Loquitur** cum amīcō.
***He is speaking*** *with his friend.*

## What is Meant by Mood?

The word mood is a variation of the word *mode*, meaning manner or way. The **MOOD** is the form of the verb which indicates the attitude (mode) of the speaker toward what he is saying. As a beginning student of Latin, all you have to know are the names of the moods so that you will understand what your Latin textbook means when it uses these words. You will learn to use the various moods as you learn the verbs and their tenses and usages.

**In English:** Verbs can be in one of three moods:

1. The **INDICATIVE MOOD** is used to express or indicate facts. This is the most common mood, and most verb forms that you use in everyday conversation belong to the indicative mood.

   Jason *brought* back the Golden Fleece.[1]
   Medea *is* Jason's helper.
   *Did* Jason also *bring* back Medea?

2. The **IMPERATIVE MOOD** is used to express a command (see p. 100).

   Jason, *bring* back the Golden Fleece!
   Medea, *be* a helper to Jason!

3. The **SUBJUNCTIVE MOOD** is frequently used to express an action that is not really occurring (see p. 102). It is the language of wish, possibility, condition, and other vague situations.

   The king insists that Jason *bring* back the Golden Fleece.
   If Medea *were* loyal, she would not betray her father.
   Medea wishes that Jason *were* her husband.

---

[1]Jason went to the land of Colchis to bring back the Golden Fleece. Medea, daughter of the king of Colchis, aided him, and he brought her back as his bride after a long journey. Eventually he left her for another woman.

**In Latin:** These same three moods exist and have their own special forms. Although the indicative is a common mood, as in English, the subjunctive is also very important in Latin. (See **What is the Subjunctive Mood?**, p. 102.) Most of the sentences you meet in the beginning of your study, however, will be in the indicative or imperative mood.

## What is the Imperative Mood?

The IMPERATIVE is the mood of the verb used for commands. It is used to give an order.

**In English:** The verb in the imperative is the same as the DICTIONARY FORM of the verb. There are two types of commands:

1. The *YOU* COMMAND is used when giving a direct order to one person or to many persons. The second person subject "you" is not stated in the command and must be understood from the situation, either singular or plural.

    Medea, *come* with me!
    Sailors, *be ready* to sail!

    In these sentences neither *Medea* nor *Sailors* is the subject, but rather the subject is "you" which must be understood with each sentence.

2. The *LET...* COMMAND is more of an invitation, given to oneself or to others. It is used for first person (*me, us*) and for third person (*him, her, them*).

*Let me* tell you about them.
*Let's (Let us)* go!
*Let him (her, them)* die!

**In Latin:** The same two forms of commands exist, but with these differences. The second person *you* command is expressed by the imperative mood, separated into singular and plural. The "Let . . . " idea is expressed by the subjunctive.

1. The second person *YOU* COMMAND uses the special form of the verb called the imperative, separated into singular and plural. Both forms are based on the present stem.

   Mēdēa, **venī** mēcum!
   imperative singular

   *Medea, **come** with me.*

   Argonautae, **venīte** mēcum!
   imperative plural

   *Argonauts, **come** with me.*[1]

   *Medea* and *Argonauts*, the persons being addressed, are in the vocative case (see p. 23).

   - Imperative singular = PRESENT STEM

   | | | |
   |---|---|---|
   | Amā! | *Love*! | [addressing one person] |
   | Docē! | *Teach*! | |

   - Imperative plural = PRESENT STEM + *-TE*

   | | | |
   |---|---|---|
   | Amāte! | *Love*! | [addressing more than one person] |
   | Docēte! | *Teach*! | |

[1]The Argonauts are the sailors on the ship, the *Argo,* who sailed with Jason in search of the Golden Fleece.

Consult your Latin textbook for the complete imperative forms.

2. The *LET*... COMMAND (*let me, let us, let him, her, it, them*) idea is expressed by the subjunctive mood.

Vīvat! *Let him live!*

## What is the Subjunctive Mood?

The subjunctive mood exists in English, but it is used only in a few situations. It occurs in:

- contrary-to-fact statements

If I *were* you, I would go on vacation.

Implication: But I am not you.

She talks as though she *were* my mother.

Implication: But she is not my mother.

- statements expressing a wish that is not possible

I wish it *were* not true.

But it is true.

I wish that she *were* my teacher.

But she is not my teacher.

- in clauses introduced by the following verbs of asking, demanding and recommending

  I recommend that he *take* the course.
  
  instead of "takes"

  I demanded that she *come* to see me.
  
  instead of "comes"

These are just a few examples to show that English has the subjunctive form, but it is not used as frequently as it is used in Latin. In all of the above situations Latin uses the subjunctive mood, and in addition there are many other uses of the subjunctive. Therefore, we refer you to the explanations and examples of the subjunctive in your Latin textbook.

**In Latin:** In general the personal endings of the present subjunctive are the same as the endings for the indicative verbs, but the vowels before the endings change to indicate the subjunctive mood. There are only four tenses for the subjunctive: present, imperfect, perfect, and past perfect (pluperfect). There is no future or future perfect tense, since the whole idea of the subjunctive is based on future uncertainty. The verbs have both the active and passive voice. Consult the paradigms in the back of your textbook for the complete forms.

## What is a Conjunction?

A CONJUNCTION is a word which joins words, phrases, or clauses (see p. 110).

> Jason *and* Medea fled from her father.[1]
> *Neither* Jason *nor* Medea remained in Colchis.
> The lovers travelled over the sea *and* through many countries.
> Medea loved Jason, *but* he left her.
> They were happy *until* Jason wanted a new wife.
> Medea killed her children *because* she hated Jason.

There are two kinds of conjunctions: coordinating and subordinating (also called coordinate and subordinate).

1. COORDINATING CONJUNCTIONS join words, phrases, and clauses that are equal; they connect or *coordinate* ideas of equal rank.

| | |
|---|---|
| Connecting words: | good *or* evil |
| Connecting phrases: | over the sea *and* through many countries |
| Connecting clauses: | The sea was rough, *but* the lovers were happy. |

2. SUBORDINATING CONJUNCTIONS join a dependent clause to the main clause; they connect one thought in a lower or *subordinate* sense to another main idea.

   Clauses introduced by subordinating conjunctions are called SUBORDINATE CLAUSES (see p. 111).

[1]See fn. p. 99.

main clause — subordinate clause

The lovers were happy *until* Jason wanted a new wife.

*until*: subordinating conjuction

subordinate clause — main clause

*Although* the sea was rough, the lovers were happy.

*Although*: subordinating conjunction

main clause — subordinate clause

Medea was angry *because* Jason left her.

*because*: subordinating conjunction

Notice that the main clause is not always the first clause of the sentence.

**In English:** The major coordinating conjunctions are *and, but, or, nor, yet,* and *for*. Typical subordinating conjunctions are *although, because, if, unless, so that, while, that,* and *whenever.* Some words like *before* and *after* function as both prepositions and subordinating conjunctions.

We can distinguish between a preposition and a subordinating conjunction simply by determining if the word introduces a prepositional phrase (see p. 109) or a subordinate clause (see p. 111).

prepositional phrase

- Medea loved Jason *before* their departure.

*before*: preposition — departure: object of preposition

subordinate clause

Medea loved Jason *before* he loved another woman.

subject verb object

subordinating conjunction

prepositional phrase

• *After* the voyage, Jason and Medea returned to Greece.

preposition object of preposition

subordinate clause

*After* the voyage was over, Jason and Medea returned to Greece.

subordinating conjunction subject verb

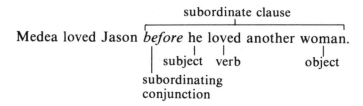

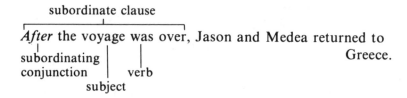

Both phrases and subordinate clauses may precede or follow the main clause.

**In Latin:** Conjunctions are to be memorized as vocabulary items. Like adverbs and prepositions, conjunctions are invariable; they never change. (They do not have case, number, gender, or tense.)

The major coordinating conjunctions are **et** (*and*), **sed** (*but*), **aut** (*or*), **neque** (*nor*), and **autem** (*however*). Typical subordinating conjunctions are **quamquam** (*although*), **quod** (*because*), **quia** (*because*), **sī** (*if*), **cum** (*when*), **ubi** (*when*), **ut** (*so that*), **dum** (*while*), and **postquam** (*after*).

You cannot assume that a word which serves as both a preposition and a subordinating conjunction in English also serves as both in Latin. Latin uses different words for each.

- Mēdēa Iāsonem amāvit **ante** discessum.

  (ante: preposition; discessum: object of preposition)

  *Medea loved Jason **before** their departure.*

  Mēdēa Iāsonem amābat **antequam** aliam fēminam amāvit.

  (antequam: subordinating conjunction; fēminam: object; amāvit: verb)

  *Medea loved Jason **before** he loved another woman.*

- **Post** nāvigātiōnem, Iāson et Mēdēa in Graeciā habitābant.

  (Post: preposition; nāvigātiōnem: object of preposition)

  ***After** the voyage, Jason and Medea lived in Greece.*

  **Postquam** nāvigātiō fīnīta est, Iāson et Mēdēa in Graeciā habitābant.

  (Postquam: subordinating conjunction; nāvigātiō: subject; fīnīta est: verb)

  ***After** the voyage was over, Jason and Medea lived in Greece.*

Some subordinating conjunctions require the use of the indicative mood for the verb which follows, others the use of the subjunctive mood. Some are followed by either mood, depending on the meaning of the sentence. When you learn a new conjunction, be sure to memorize what mood it governs.

## What are Sentences, Phrases and Clauses?

### What is a sentence?

A **SENTENCE** is the expression of a thought usually consisting at least of a subject (see **What is a Subject?**, p. 24) and a verb (see **What is a Verb?**, p. 50).

Atalanta lost.
subject verb

The people were cheering.
subject verb phrase

How did Hippomenes win?[1]
subject
verb phrase

Depending on the verb, a sentence may also have direct and indirect objects (see **What are Objects?**, p. 31).

Atalanta lost the race.
subject verb direct object

The king gave him the reward.
subject verb indirect object direct object

In addition, a sentence may include various kinds of modifiers: adjectives (see **What is an Adjective?**, p. 130), adverbs (see **What is an Adverb?**, p. 158), prepositional phrases (see **What is a Preposition?**, p. 187), participial phrases (see **What is a Participle?**, p. 80).

[1]All the young men who wanted to marry Atalanta had to race with her. Hippomenes distracted Atalanta by throwing three golden apples, one at a time, along the course, thereby winning the race and a bride.

Atalanta lost the race.

subject — verb — direct object

Atalanta lost the *long* race.

adjective

*Eventually* Atalanta lost the long race.

adverb

Eventually Atalanta lost the long race *because of her curiosity.*

preposition phrase

Eventually Atalanta, *delayed by the apples,* lost the long race

participial phrase modifying *Atalanta*

because of her curiosity.

Although not all of these elements of a sentence occur in Latin in the same way that they do in English, you will find it very helpful to recognize all the different parts of a sentence in each language. Moreover, it will be important for you to recognize complete sentences and to distinguish phrases and clauses from complete sentences.

## What is a phrase?

A **PHRASE** is a group of two or more words expressing a thought, but without a subject or a conjugated verb. It may contain an object. The various phrases are identified by the type of word beginning the phrase.

- **PREPOSITIONAL PHRASE**: starts with a *preposition*

*along* the way

preposition — object of preposition

*after* the race
preposition — object of preposition

*towards* the end
preposition — object of preposition

- **PARTICIPIAL PHRASE**: starts with a *participle*

*throwing* the apple
present participle of *throw* — object of *throwing*

*thrown* to the side
past participle of *throw* — prepositional phrase used adverbially telling where, modifying *thrown*

- **INFINITIVE PHRASE**: starts with an *infinitive*

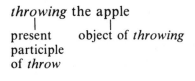

*to learn* Latin
infinitive — object of *to learn*

*to win* the race dishonestly
infinitive — adverb modifying *to win*

To recognize such phrases you need to recognize the individual parts (prepositions, participles, infinitives) and then isolate all those words within groups of words which work as a unit of meaning. If this unit of meaning does not have both a subject and a conjugated verb, it is a phrase.

## What is a clause?

A **CLAUSE** is a group of words containing a subject and a conjugated verb. It forms part of a compound or complex sentence (see p. 113).

There are two kinds of clauses: main (or independent) and subordinate (or dependent).

1. A **MAIN CLAUSE** generally expresses a complete thought, the important idea of the sentence. If it stood alone with a capitalized first word and a period at the end, it could be a simple sentence. It is called a main clause only when it is part of a larger sentence.

2. A **SUBORDINATE CLAUSE** cannot stand alone as a complete sentence. It must always be combined with a main clause.

main clause / subordinate clause

Hippomenes won the race because Atalanta was curious.

subject (Hippomenes), verb (won) / subject (Atalanta), verb (was)

main clause / subordinate clause

Atalanta lost the race when she picked up the last apple.

subject (Atalanta), verb (lost) / subject (she), verb (picked)

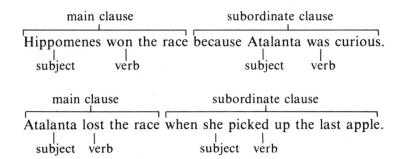

These sentences containing a main clause and a subordinate clause are called **COMPLEX SENTENCES** (see p. 114).

Let us look at the three types of sentences: simple, compound and complex.

A. A **SIMPLE SENTENCE** is one consisting of only one main clause with no subordinate clause. It has a subject and a conjugated verb. There may be many modifiers with a variety of word order.

**In English:** There is no set position for the verb in an English sentence or clause, but the subject usually comes before the verb, except in questions.

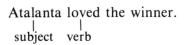

Atalanta loved the winner.

subject (Atalanta), verb (loved)

Some other modifier can come before the subject.

*Secretly* Atalanta loved the winner.
adverb

prepositional phrase modifying *loved* telling when
Even *before the race* Atalanta secretly loved the winner.

In questions, the word order varies from the normal simple sentence order.

Did Atalanta love Hippomenes?
subject
verb phrase

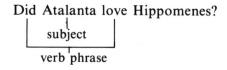

In spite of the many modifiers, all of the above are simple sentences.

**In Latin:** In a simple declarative sentence (a statement), the conjugated verb usually stands last in the sentence. The subject usually stands near the beginning. This word order may vary, however, according to which words are being stressed and the verb may even stand first. Remember that the endings indicate the relationship of words and ideas in the sentence (see p. 16).

Atalanta victōrem **amābat**.
subject object verb

*Atalanta* ***loved*** *the winner.*

A variety of word order is possible depending on what is being stressed.

- **Clam** Atalanta victōrem amābat.
  adverb subject verb

  ***Secretly*** *Atalanta loved the winner.*

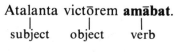

- ***Even before the race*** *Atalanta loved the winner.*
  **Etiam ante certāmen** Atalanta victōrem amābat.

  The time element, "even before the race," is being stressed.

- **Victōrem** Atalanta etiam ante certāmen amābat.

  *The winner* is being stressed. Atalanta loved him and not someone else.

In a question, the ending **-ne** is usually attached to the verb, and since the verb is such a strong element in the sentence, it may stand first.

**Amābatne** Atalanta victōrem etiam ante certāmen?
verb + **ne**

***Did*** *Atalanta* ***love*** *the winner even before the race?*

In spite of the modifiers, the above are all simple sentences.

B. A COMPOUND SENTENCE consists of two statements or equal main clauses. These two statements are joined by coordinating conjunctions (see **What is a Conjunction?**, p. 104).

**In English:** The two main clauses are connected by a coordinating conjunction (see p. 104). Each clause has its own subject and conjugated verb. Each, standing alone, could be a simple sentence.

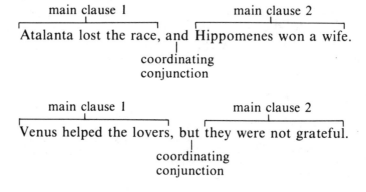

main clause 1 — main clause 2
Atalanta lost the race, and Hippomenes won a wife.
and — coordinating conjunction

main clause 1 — main clause 2
Venus helped the lovers, but they were not grateful.
but — coordinating conjunction

**In Latin:** As in English, the two main clauses are connected by a coordinating conjunction.

main clause — main clause

Venus amantēs **iūvit**, sed hī nōn grātī **erant**.

subject — verb — coordinating conjunction — subject — verb

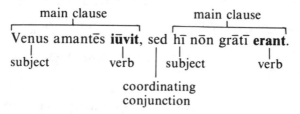

*Venus* ***aided*** *the lovers, but they* ***were*** *not grateful.*

C. A **COMPLEX SENTENCE** is a sentence consisting of a main clause and one or more subordinate clauses.

The **MAIN CLAUSE** (or independent clause) in a complex sentence generally can stand alone as a complete sentence.[1]

The **SUBORDINATE CLAUSE** (or dependent clause) cannot stand alone as a complete sentence; it depends on the main clause for its full meaning, and it is subordinate to the main clause.

subordinate clause — main clause

Although the lovers were happy, Venus was angry.

subordinate conjunction — subject — verb — subject — verb

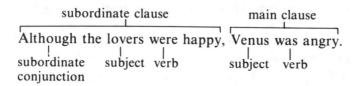

It makes sense to say "Venus was angry" without the first clause in the sentence; therefore, it is a main clause and could stand alone, independent of the "although" idea. It does not make sense to say "although the lovers were happy" unless we add a conclusion; therefore, it is a subordinate clause.

[1]Sometimes the main clause, though grammatically complete since it has a subject and a conjugated verb, cannot stand alone as a complete thought: *Hippomenes hoped that he would win.* "Hippomenes hoped" is incomplete without the subordinate clause telling what he hoped. Most main clauses, however, do express a complete thought.

**In English:** It is important that you be able to distinguish a main clause from a subordinate clause. To do so will help you to write complete sentences and avoid sentence fragments. Subordinate clauses are introduced by subordinate conjunctions (see p. 111) and by relative pronouns (see p. 179).

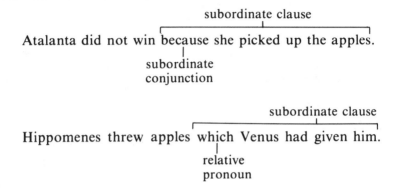

subordinate clause

Atalanta did not win because she picked up the apples.

subordinate conjunction

subordinate clause

Hippomenes threw apples which Venus had given him.

relative pronoun

**In Latin:** The distinction between the main clause and the subordinate clause is just as important as it is in English, and the same elements are involved.

In the main clause (which can stand first or last) the verb again is usually last in the sentence unless other words are being emphasized. The linking verb, however, does not necessarily stand last.

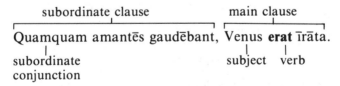

subordinate clause | main clause

Quamquam amantēs gaudēbant, Venus **erat** īrāta.

subordinate conjunction | subject | verb

*Although the lovers were happy, Venus* ***was*** *angry.*

As in English, subordinate clauses may be introduced by subordinate conjunctions and by relative pronouns.

main clause | subordinate clause

Atalanta certāmine nōn superāvit **quod** pōma carpsit.

subject — verb — subordinate conjunction

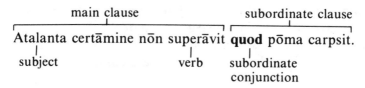

*Atalanta did not win the race **because** she picked up the apples.*

main clause | subordinate clause

Hippomenēs dēiēcit tria pōma aurea **quae** Venus eī dederat.

subject — verb — relative pronoun

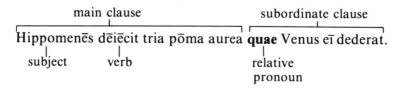

*Hippomenes threw the three golden apples **which** Venus had given him.*

The verb in the subordinate clause can be in the indicative or subjunctive mood (see **What is the Subjunctive Mood?**, p. 102, and **What is a Conjunction?**, p. 104).

Some clauses introduced by "that" following verbs of saying, knowing, thinking, feeling and the like, do not have verbs in either indicative or subjunctive; they have verbs in the infinitive. (See **What is Meant by Direct and Indirect Statement?**, p. 119.)

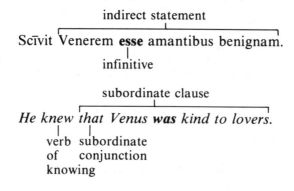

indirect statement

Scīvit Venerem **esse** amantibus benignam.

infinitive

subordinate clause

*He knew that Venus **was** kind to lovers.*

verb of knowing — subordinate conjunction

**What are Declarative and Interrogative Sentences?**

Sentences are classified according to their purpose. A **DECLARATIVE SENTENCE** is a sentence that makes a statement.

The Greeks invaded Troy.[1]

An **INTERROGATIVE SENTENCE** is a sentence that asks a question.

Why did the Greeks invade Troy?

In written language, an interrogative sentence always has a question mark at the end.

**In English:** To change a statement (**S**) into a question (**Q**), you sometimes need the helping verb (auxiliary) *do/does/did/is/are/was/were* before the subject. The verb may change into a participle. The auxiliary verb serves to alert you that what follows is a question.

S: The Greek leaders invaded Troy.
Q: *Did* the Greek leaders invade Troy?
Q: *Were* the Greek leaders invading Troy?

S: Paris carried off the beautiful Helen.
Q: *Did* Paris carry off the beautiful Helen?

Another way to make a question is to switch the verb and the subject around, placing the verb before the subject. This reversing of the normal "subject + verb" order is called inverting or **INVERSION.**

S: *The Greeks are* now in Troy.
Q: *Are the Greeks* now in Troy?

[1]The Trojan War was fought to bring back the beautiful Helen from Troy, where she had been taken by Paris, a Trojan prince. The Greeks built the Trojan Horse as a device to enter the city and capture it.

**In Latin:** Statements can be changed into questions by using the following methods:

S: Ducēs Graecī Trōiam invādēbant.
*The Greek leaders were invading Troy.*

1. Adding **-ne** to the first word in the sentence. The answer can be either "yes" or "no."

   Q: **Invādēbantne** Trōiam ducēs Graecī?
   ***Were** the Greek leaders **invading** Troy?*

   Often the verb appears first in a question, since it is the word being stressed in the sentence.

2. Introducing the sentence with **Nōnne**. In this way a "yes" answer is expected.

   Q: **Nōnne** Graecī Trōiam invāsērunt?
   ***Did** the Greeks **not** invade Troy?*
   [Expected answer: "Yes."]

   or

   *The Greeks invaded Troy, **didn't they**?*

3. Introducing the sentence with **Num**. In this way a "no" answer is expected.

   Q: **Num** Graecī Rōmam invāsērunt?
   *The Greeks did **not** invade Rome, **did they**?*
   [Expected answer: "No."]

Questions can be introduced by a variety of interrogative words: **Quōmodo** (*how*), **ubi** (*where*), **quandō** (*when*), **cūr** (*why*), **quis** (*who*), etc.

Q: **Cūr** Graecī Trōiam invāserunt?
***Why** did the Greeks invade Troy?*

Q: **Quandō** Paris Helenam abripuit?
*__When__ did Paris carry off Helen?*

Q: **Quōmodo** Graecī Trōiam vīcērunt?
*__How__ did the Greeks conquer Troy?*

Q: **Quis** Helenam abripuit?
*__Who__ carried off Helen?*

## What is Meant by Direct and Indirect Statement?

DIRECT STATEMENT is the transmission of a message by direct quotation. The message is set in quotation marks.

> Caesar says, *"I came, I saw, I conquered."*
> Cicero said, *"My city is in danger."*

INDIRECT STATEMENT is the reporting of the message without quoting the words directly. It does not use quotation marks.

> Caesar says *that he came, he saw, he conquered.*
> Cicero said *that his city was in danger.*

Notice in the first sentence above how the speaker's first person pronoun ("*I* came . . . ") in the direct statement changes to agree logically with the perspective of the person doing the reporting in indirect statement ("*he* came . . . "). Also, in the second sentence the possessive adjective "My" has changed to "his."

**In English:** Indirect statement is easy to recognize since the reported message is introduced by "that" forming a subordinate clause (see

p. 111) used as an object of the verb of saying. No quotation marks are used.

> Caesar says *that he came, he saw, he conquered.*
> Cicero said *that his city was in danger.*

When the direct statement is transformed into a reported message, there is usually a shift in tense to maintain the logical time sequence in indirect statement.

| Direct Statement | → | Indirect Statement |
|---|---|---|
| | | main clause / subordinate clause |
| Cicero *said* (past), "My city *is* (present) in danger." | | Cicero *said* (past) that his city *was* (past) in danger. |
| Cicero *said* (past), "My city *was* (past) in danger." | | Cicero *said* (past) that his city *had been* (past perfect) in danger. |
| Cicero *said* (past), "My city *will be* (future) in danger." | | Cicero *said* (past) that his city *would be* (auxiliary *would* + verb) in danger. |

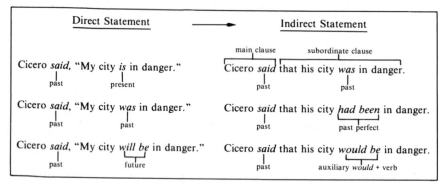

**In Latin:** The construction of indirect statement is used not only after verbs of saying, but also after verbs of thinking, feeling, sensing, and the like. The word "that" which appears in English is omitted in Latin. Indirect statement is very commonly used in Latin and follows special rules distinct from direct statement.

- The subject of the indirect statement is in the accusative case.[1]

- The verb of the indirect statement is an infinitive.

Compare the direct statements to the indirect statements below:

---

[1]In English the subject of an infinitive is also in the objective case (Latin = accusative): "I want *him* to love me," "We invited *them* to come," or "I consider *her* to be the best in the class."

| Direct Statement | Indirect Statement |
| --- | --- |
| Caesar dīcit, "**Vēnī, vīdī, vīcī.**"<br>verbs = indicative | Caesar dīcit **sē vēnisse, vīdisse, vīcisse.**<br>subject = accusative; verbs = infinitive |
| *Caesar says,* ***"I came, I saw, I conquered."*** | *Caesar says* ***that he came, he saw, he conquered.*** |
| Cicero dixit, "**Mea urbs est** in perīculō."<br>subject = nominative; verb = indicative | Cicero dixit **suam urbem esse** in perīculō.<br>subject = accusative; verb = infinitive |
| *Cicero said, "**My city is** in danger."* | *Cicero said **that his city was** in danger.* |

Remember that there are three tenses of infinitives in Latin: present, perfect, and future (see **What is an Infinitive?**, p. 55). The infinitive tense selected for the indirect statement depends on when the action of the subordinate clause occurred relative to the action of the main verb.

- present infinitive = action of subordinate clause at same time as main verb

  Cicero **putat** urbem suam **esse** in perīculō.
  present indicative — present infinitive

  *Cicero **thinks** that his city **is in danger.***

- perfect infinitive = action of subordinate clause before time of main verb

  Cicero **putat** urbem suam **fuisse** in perīculō.
  present indicative — perfect infinitive

  *Cicero **thinks** that his city **was in danger.***

- future infinitive = action of subordinate clause after action of main verb

  Cicero **putat** urbem suam **futūram esse** in perīculō.
  present indicative — future infinitive

  *Cicero **thinks** that his city **will be** in danger.*

The English translation changes for these same three Latin infinitives when the tense of the verb in the main clause is in the past time. The change is necessary to maintain the time relationship between the main and subordinate clauses, but note that the Latin infinitive does not change.

Cicero **putāvit** urbem suam **esse** in perīculō.
perfect indicative — present infinitive

*Cicero* ***thought*** *that his city* ***was*** *in danger.*

Cicero **putāvit** urbem suam **fuisse** in perīculō.
perfect indicative — perfect infinitive

*Cicero* ***thought*** *that his city* ***had been*** *in danger.*

Cicero **putāvit** urbem suam **futūram esse** in perīculō.
perfect indicative — future infinitive

*Cicero* ***thought*** *that his city* ***would be*** *in danger.*

Consult your text for a complete discussion of indirect statement.

## What is Meant by Direct and Indirect Question?

DIRECT QUESTION is the transmission of a question by direct quotation. The question is set in quotation marks.

> Paris asks, *"Where is Helen?"*
> Helen wondered, *"When are the Greeks coming?"*
> Priam asked, *"Who are the Greek leaders?"*
> Paris wondered, *"How did I fail?"*

INDIRECT QUESTION is the reporting of a question without using the exact words of the speaker. It does not use quotation marks nor end in a question mark, since the direct question has become part of a sentence that is no longer a question. It follows verbs of asking, knowing, doubting, wondering, and the like.

> Paris asked *where Helen was.*
> Helen wondered *when the Greek leaders were coming.*
> Priam asked *who the Greek leaders were.*
> Paris wondered *how he had failed.*

The word order is adjusted and any pronouns are logically changed to agree with the perspective of the person asking or wondering in the main clause.

**In English:** An indirect question is easy to recognize since the quoted question has become a subordinate clause introduced by the same interrogative word (*why, where, who, what, when,* etc.) that introduced the direct question.

There is often a shift in tense in the subordinate clause when the main verb is in the past tense.

| Direct Question → | Indirect Question |
|---|---|
| Priam *asked*, "Who *are* the Greek leaders?" | Priam *asked* who the Greek leaders *were*. |
| past — present | past — past |
| Paris *asked*, "Where *was* Helen?" | Paris *asked* where Helen *had been*. |
| past — past | past — pluperfect |
| Paris *wondered*, "How *did* I *fail?*" | Paris *wondered* how he *had failed*. |
| past — past | past — pluperfect |

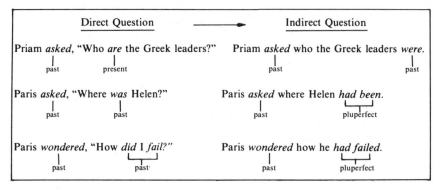

**In Latin:** An indirect question is easy to recognize since the quoted question has become a subordinate clause introduced by the same interrogative word (**cūr**, *why*; **quis**, *who*; **quid**, *what*; **quandō**, *when*; **ubi**, *where*; **quōmodo**, *how*; etc.) that introduced the direct question. Indirect questions are very common in Latin and follow special rules distinct from direct questions.

- The verb of the indirect question is in the subjunctive mood.

- The tenses of the verbs follow a pattern known as **SEQUENCE OF TENSES** divided into PRIMARY SEQUENCE (when the main verb is in the present or future tense) and SECONDARY SEQUENCE (when the main verb is in any past tense).

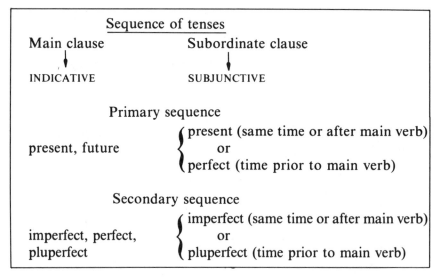

Sequence of tenses

| Main clause | Subordinate clause |
|---|---|
| INDICATIVE | SUBJUNCTIVE |
| **Primary sequence** | |
| present, future | present (same time or after main verb)<br>or<br>perfect (time prior to main verb) |
| **Secondary sequence** | |
| imperfect, perfect, pluperfect | imperfect (same time or after main verb)<br>or<br>pluperfect (time prior to main verb) |

Let us see how this table works in practice.

| Direct Question → | Indirect Question |
|---|---|
| **Primary Sequence** | |
| Paris **rogat**, "Ubi **est** Helena?" | Paris **rogat** ubi Helena **sit**. |
| rogat: present indicative; est: present indicative | rogat: present indicative; sit: present subjunctive |
| *Paris **asks**, "Where **is** Helen?"* | *Paris **asks** where Helen **is**.* |
| **Secondary Sequence** | |
| Paris **rogāvit**, "Ubi **est** Helena?" | Paris **rogāvit** ubi Helena **esset**. |
| rogāvit: perfect indicative; est: present indicative | rogāvit: perfect indicative; esset: imperfect subjunctive |
| *Paris **asked**, "Where **is** Helen?"* | *Paris **asked** where Helen **was**.* |
| Paris **rogāvit**, "Ubi **erat** Helena?" | Paris **rogāvit** ubi Helena **fuisset**. |
| rogāvit: perfect indicative; erat: imperfect indicative | rogāvit: perfect indicative; fuisset: pluperfect subjunctive |
| *Paris **asked**, "Where **was** Helen?"* | *Paris **asked** where Helen **had been**.* |

Remember that there are only four subjunctive tenses in Latin: present, perfect, imperfect and pluperfect (see **What is the Subjunctive Mood?**, p. 102). The subjunctive tense selected for the indirect question depends on two factors:

a. the tense of the main verb (which remains in the indicative mood)
b. the action of the verb of the subordinate clause relative to the action of the main verb.

It is very important to learn the Sequence of Tenses table, since it is used in many subjunctive constructions, not only in indirect question. It is really very logical and consistent.

## What are Conditional Sentences?

**CONDITIONAL SENTENCES** are complex sentences (see p. 114) consisting of two parts:

1. the **CONDITION**, a subordinate clause introduced by ***if*** **(sī)** or ***unless*** **(nisi**, *if... not*)
2. the **CONCLUSION** (or result of the condition), the main clause

condition — subordinate clause: If you touch the flame,
conclusion (result) — main clause: you will be burned.

If you touch the flame, you will be burned.

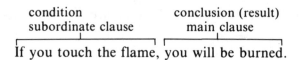

**In English:** There are three types of conditional sentences.

1. **SIMPLE CONDITIONS**—The condition can take place in present, past, or future.

Present: If you *say* this, you *are mistaken.*
*say* — present; *are mistaken* — present

Past: If you *said* this, you *were mistaken.*
*said* — past; *were mistaken* — past

Future: If you *say* this, you *will be mistaken.*
*say* — present; *will be mistaken* — future

Although the present tense is used, a future time is implied.

*Unless* can be substituted for an *if... not* condition.

*Unless* you come, the man will die.

means the same thing as:

*If* you do *not* come, the man will die.

2. *SHOULD—WOULD* **CONDITIONS**—Some doubt is implied about the possibility of the condition occurring, as expressed by the "should" in the condition and "would" in the conclusion.

If you *should* say this, you *would* be mistaken.

3. **CONTRARY-TO-FACT CONDITIONS**—There is no possibility of the condition actually occurring; as the name implies, the condition is contrary-to-fact. These statements can be made about the present or past.

Present: If my friend *were* here, I would be happy.
*were* → subjunctive

Implication: My friend is not here.
*Were* is an example of one of the rare uses of the subjunctive in English (see **What is the Subjunctive Mood?**, p. 102).

Past: If my friend *had been* here, I would have been happy.
*had been* → past perfect indicative

Implication: My friend was not here.

**In Latin:** The same three types of conditional sentences exist with almost the same sequence of tense.

1. Simple Conditions—the indicative mood is used in both clauses in any tense.

• Sī hoc **dīcis, errās**.
**dīcis** → present indicative; **errās** → present indicative

*If you* ***say*** *this, you* ***are mistaken***.
***say*** → present; ***are mistaken*** → present

- Sī hoc **dixistī, errāvistī.**

  dixistī: perfect indicative; errāvistī: perfect indicative

  *If you **said** this, you **were mistaken**.*

  said: past; were mistaken: past

- Sī hoc **dixeris, errābis**.

  dixeris: future perfect indicative; errābis: future indicative

  *If you **say** this, you **will be mistaken**.*

  say: present (1); will be mistaken: future (2)

  Although the English present tense is used for action (1), a future time is implied (see p. 74). Since action (1) will take place before action (2) in the future, in Latin action (1) must be in the future perfect tense and action (2) must be in the future. (See **What is the Future Perfect Tense?**, p. 73).

**Nisi** (*if... not*) can be used to translate *unless*.

**Nisi** cito vēneris, homō moriētur.

vēneris: future perfect indicative; moriētur: future indicative

***Unless** you come quickly, the man will die.*

2. *Should... would* clauses—the subjunctive mood is used in both clauses. As in English, so in Latin, this condition implies some doubt about the condition occurring.

Sī hoc **dīcās, errēs**.

dīcās: present subjunctive; errēs: present subjunctive

*If you **should say** this, you **would be mistaken**.*

3. Contrary-to-fact conditions—the subjunctive mood is used in both clauses. As in English, here also, there is no possibility of the condition occurring.

Present: Sī amīcus meus nunc **adesset**, laetus **essem**.

**adesset** — imperfect subjunctive; **essem** — imperfect subjunctive

*If my friend* ***were here*** *now,* ***I would be*** *happy.*

Past: Sī amīcus meus heri **adfuisset**, laetus **fuissem**.

**adfuisset** — pluperfect subjunctive; **fuissem** — pluperfect subjunctive

*If my friend* ***had been here*** *yesterday,* ***I would have been*** *happy.*

## What is an Adjective?

An ADJECTIVE is a word that describes a noun or pronoun. Be sure that you do not confuse an adjective with a pronoun. A pronoun replaces a noun, while an adjective must always have a noun or pronoun to describe.

There are different types of adjectives. Each type is studied in a section of this handbook. Listed below are the various categories and the section where they are discussed.

**In English:** Adjectives describe nouns in many ways. They indicate:

- what kind of noun it is—DESCRIPTIVE ADJECTIVE (see p. 131)

  Penelope lived in a *large* house.
  The stars are *bright.*

- whose noun it is—POSSESSIVE ADJECTIVE (see p. 146)

  Aeneas loved *his* mother.
  Venus often gave comfort to *her* son.

- which noun it is—INTERROGATIVE ADJECTIVE (see p. 151)

  *What* goddess did Niobe offend?
  *Which* child died last?

- which noun is indicated—DEMONSTRATIVE ADJECTIVE (see p. 154)

  Cicero formed *this* plan.
  *That* senator praised the orator.

- a noun which is not clearly indicated—INDEFINITE ADJECTIVE

  *Some* Trojans escaped from the city.
  Did *any* hope of safety remain?

Since the use of the indefinite adjective in Latin closely corresponds to the English use, there is no special section devoted to this type of adjective. The Latin indefinite adjectives, however, have degrees of uncertainty which can easily be learned from your textbook.

In all the sentences above, it is said that the adjective *modifies* the noun.

**In Latin:** Adjectives also describe nouns and pronouns in various ways. The main difference with English is that in Latin the adjective always agrees with the noun or pronoun it modifies; that is, the ending of the adjective reflects the same case, gender and number as the noun it describes.

## What is a Descriptive Adjective?

A DESCRIPTIVE ADJECTIVE is a word which describes a noun or pronoun.

**In English:** The descriptive adjective does not change form, regardless of the noun or pronoun it modifies.

He has *bright* eyes.
The *bright* star is beautiful.
The farmer lives in a *large* house.
We are looking at the *large* temple.

Descriptive adjectives are divided into two groups depending on how they accompany the noun they modify:

1. An **ATTRIBUTIVE ADJECTIVE** usually precedes the noun it modifies.

   She lived in a *large* house.
   We are looking at the *bright* star.
   They have a *kind* teacher.

2. A **PREDICATE ADJECTIVE** follows a linking verb: *be, seem, appear, become,* etc. (see p. 27); it refers back to the subject.

   The house appears *large.*
   The stars are *bright.*
   The teacher seems *kind.*

**In Latin:** Like all adjectives in Latin, a descriptive adjective always agrees with the noun or pronoun it modifies; that is, the ending of the adjective reflects the same case, gender and number as the word it describes. Descriptive adjectives generally follow the nouns they modify, but adjectives of size and quantity precede.

Oculōs **clārōs** habet.
acc. masc. pl.

*He has* ***bright*** *eyes.*

Stella **clāra** est pulchra.
nom. fem. sing.

*The* ***bright*** *star is beautiful.*

Agricola in **magnā** casā habitat.
abl. fem. sing.

*The farmer lives in a* ***large*** *hut.*

**Magnum** templum spectāmus.
acc. neut. sing.

*We are looking at the* ***large*** *temple.*

The gender, number and case of an adjective depend on the noun it modifies; the ending of the adjective depends on the declension to which the adjective belongs.

- adjectives of the first and second declension merge into a single group (called Group A in this handbook)

- adjectives of the third declension (called Group B in this handbook)

When you meet an adjective in the vocabulary, see whether it has one, two, or three endings. If it has the **-us,**[1] **-a, -um** endings, it belongs to Group A. All the others belong to Group B.

Group A: Adjectives of the first and second declension

- Most of these adjectives are identifiable by their three-form entry in the vocabulary or dictionary ending in **-us, -a, -um.**

Dictionary entry: bonus, -a, -um *good*

Fully written: bonus, bona, bonum
masc. fem. neut.

The masculine and neuter forms, **bonus** and **bonum**, are second declension; the feminine **bona** forms are first declension.

| | Singular | | | Plural | | |
|---|---|---|---|---|---|---|
| | Masc. | Fem. | Neut. | Masc. | Fem. | Neut. |
| Nom. | bonus | bona | bonum | bonī | bonae | bona |
| Gen. | bonī | bonae | bonī | bonōrum | bonārum | bonōrum |
| Dat. | bonō | bonae | bonō | bonīs | bonīs | bonīs |
| Acc. | bonum | bonam | bonum | bonōs | bonās | bona |
| Abl. | bonō | bonā | bonō | bonīs | bonīs | bonīs |

[1]Or **-er** for an adjective like **miser, misera, miserum.**

- There are several adjectives following this pattern whose nominative masculine singular ends in **-er**. Whether these adjectives keep or drop the **-e-** in the stem is apparent in the feminine and neuter forms given in the vocabulary entry. The rest of the declension is completely regular.

| | Keep the **-e-** | Drop the **-e-** |
|---|---|---|
| Dictionary entry: | **miser**, -a, -um | **pul**cher, -**chr**a, -**chr**um |
| Stem: | miser- | pulchr- |

Group B: Adjectives of the third declension

- Most of the adjectives belonging to this group have two forms: the first for the masculine and feminine genders, and the second for the neuter.

| | | | |
|---|---|---|---|
| Dictionary entry: | fidēlis, -e | | *faithful* |
| Fully written: | fidēlis<br>masc.<br>fem. | fidēle<br>neut. | |

- Some adjectives in this group have one form for all three genders. Since the stem of the adjective is not always seen in the nominative singular form, the dictionary entry also includes the complete genitive form.

| | | | |
|---|---|---|---|
| Dictionary entry: | audax<br>masc.<br>fem.<br>neut. | **audācis**<br>gen. | *bold* |

**Audāc**- is the stem of the adjective to which the endings are added.

- Some other adjectives in this group have three forms, one for each gender. They can be distinguished from the three-form adjectives of Group A because they do not have the group's **-a, -um** endings for the feminine and neuter genders. If the stem of the adjective is not seen in the nominative singular, the dictionary entry gives the complete feminine and neuter forms.

| Dictionary entry: | ācer | **ācr**is | **ācr**e | *sharp* |
|---|---|---|---|---|
| | masc. | fem. | neut. | |

**Ācr-** is the stem of the adjective to which the endings are added.

Remember that all the adjectives in Group B follow the third declension. Consult your textbook for the complete declension of the adjectives in Group B.

You must be thoroughly familiar with your case endings, since an adjective from one declension may modify a noun from another declension. Remember, the adjective must agree with its noun in case, gender and number, but its endings may be different.

In **magnīs urbibus** habitāmus.

| magnīs | urbibus |
|---|---|
| 2nd decl. | 3rd decl. |
| abl.fem.pl. | abl.fem.pl. |

*We live in **large cities**.*

Here is a chart you can use to determine the declension to which an adjective belongs on the basis of the number of forms listed in the nominative singular.

| Group | No. of forms | Declension | Nominative singular: Masculine | Feminine | Neuter |
|---|---|---|---|---|---|
| A | 3 | 1st | | bon**a**<br>miser**a** | |
| | | 2nd | bon**us**<br>miser | | bon**um**<br>miser**um** |
| | 3 | | ācer | ācr**is** | ācr**e** |
| B | 2 | 3rd | fidēl**is** | → | fidēl**e** |
| | 1 | | auda**x** | → | → |

To make sure that your adjective has the proper ending, follow these steps:

1. Analyze the noun it modifies:

   - case

     Is it nominative, genitive, dative, accusative or ablative?

   - gender

     Is it masculine, feminine or neuter?

   - number

     Is it singular or plural?

2. Determine the declension of the adjective.

3. Choose the form (case-ending) of the adjective which corresponds to the case, gender and number of the noun.

Remember: The adjective agrees with the noun it modifies in case, gender and number, but it does not always have the same ending.

Here are a few examples to show you how to apply the three steps above:

- *Cicero was a* ***true*** *orator.*

  1. Analysis of noun *orator:* **ōrātor**
     Case: nominative
     Gender: masculine
     Number: singular
  2. Declension of adjective *true*
     Dictionary entry: **vērus, -a, -um**
     Gender of adjective: masculine since **ōrātor** is masculine noun.
     Declension: **vērus** = masculine Group A second declension
  3. Case ending and number of **vērus:**
     **Ōrātor** is nominative singular =
     **vērus** must be in the nominative singular.

  Cicero erat ōrātor **vērus.**

  nom. masc. sing.

- *Friends will aid the* ***unfortunate*** *neighbors.*

  1. Analysis of noun *neighbors:* **vīcīnōs**
     Case: accusative
     Gender: masculine
     Number: plural
  2. Declension of adjective *unfortunate*
     Dictionary entry: **miser, -a, -um**
     Gender of adjective: masculine since **vīcīnōs** is masculine noun.
     Declension: **miser** = masculine Group A second declension
  3. Case ending and number of **miser**:
     **Vīcīnōs** is accusative plural =
     **miser** must be in the accusative plural.

  Amīcī vīcīnōs **miserōs** iuvābunt.

  acc. masc. pl.

- *The* ***bold*** *Amazons terrified the men.*

  1. Analysis of noun *Amazons:* **Amāzonēs**
     Case: nominative
     Gender: feminine
     Number: plural
  2. Declension of adjective *bold*
     Dictionary entry: **audax, audācis** (genitive)
     Gender of adjective: feminine since **Amāzonēs** is feminine noun.
     Declension: **audax** = feminine Group B third declension
  3. Case ending and number of **audax:**
     **Amāzonēs** is nominative plural =
     **audax** must be in the nominative plural.

  Amāzonēs **audācēs** virōs terruērunt.

  nom. fem. pl.

- *Ulysses loved his* ***faithful*** *queen.*

  1. Analysis of noun *queen:* **rēgīnam**
     Case: accusative
     Gender: feminine
     Number: singular

2. Declension of adjective *faithful*
   Dictionary entry: **fidēlis, -e**
   Gender of adjective: feminine since **rēgīnam** is feminine noun.
   Declension: **fidēlis** = feminine Group B third declension
3. Case ending and number of **fidēlis:**
   **Rēgīnam** is accusative singular =
   **fidēlis** must be in the accusative singular.

Ulixēs rēgīnam **fidēlem** amābat.
acc. fem. sing.

- *Medusa was killed with a* ***sharp*** *sword.*

1. Analysis of noun *sword:* **gladiō**
   Case: ablative
   Gender: masculine
   Number: singular
2. Declension of adjective *sharp*
   Dictionary entry: **ācer, ācris, ācre**
   Gender of adjective: masculine since *gladiō* is masculine noun.
   Declension: **ācer** = masculine Group B third declension
3. Case ending and number of **ācer:**
   **Gladiō** is ablative singular =
   **ācer** must be in the ablative singular.

Medūsa gladiō **ācrī** necāta est.
abl. masc. sing.

As in English, there are attributive and predicate descriptive adjectives.

1. Attributive adjectives, in general, follow the nouns they modify. However, adjectives of size, quantity and number generally precede their nouns.

- **Omnēs** virī **bonī** patriam amant.

adjective noun adjective

The adjective **omnēs** belongs to the category of adjectives which precede the noun, while the adjective **bonī** belongs to the category of adjectives which follow the noun.

***All good*** *men love their country.*

Your Latin textbook will explain the position of the adjective in relation to its noun. When you use an attributive adjective be sure to check to which category it belongs.

2. Predicate adjectives modify nouns which are the subject of their sentence or their clause. Consequently, they will always be in the same case as the subject.

- nominative in most instances (see p. 27)

Stellae sunt **splendidae.**

noun — predicate adjective

nom. fem. pl.

*The stars are **bright**.*

Magister vidētur **benignus.**

noun — predicate adjective

nom. masc. sing.

*The teacher seems **kind**.*

- accusative for indirect statements (see p. 120)

Dixit gladiōs esse **ācrēs.**

noun — predicate adjective

acc. masc. pl.

*He said that the swords were **sharp**.*

## What is Meant by Comparison of Adjectives?

When adjectives are used to compare the qualities of the nouns they modify, they change forms. This change is called **COMPARISON.**

comparison of adjectives

The moon is *bright* but the sun is *brighter.*

adjective modifying the noun *moon* — adjective modifying the noun *sun*

There are three degrees of comparison: positive, comparative and superlative.

**In English:** Let us go over what is meant by the different degrees of comparison and how each degree is formed.

1. The **POSITIVE FORM** refers to the quality of one person or thing. It is simply the adjective form.

   The philosopher is *wise.*
   The moon is *bright.*
   The sword is *expensive.*
   His speech is *interesting.*

2. The **COMPARATIVE FORM** compares the quality of one person or thing with another person or thing. It is formed:

   - by adding ***-er*** to short adjectives

     The philosopher is *wiser* than many men.
     The sun is *brighter* than the moon.

   - by placing ***more*** in front of longer adjectives

     This sword is *more expensive.*
     This orator's speech is *more interesting.*

3. The **SUPERLATIVE FORM** is used to stress the highest degree of a quality. It is formed:

   - by adding ***-est*** to short adjectives

     This philosopher is the *wisest* in Athens.
     The sun is the *brightest* star in our heavens.

   - by placing ***the most*** or ***very*** in front of longer adjectives

     This sword is *the most expensive* in Rome.
     Cicero's speech is *very interesting.*

A few adjectives do not follow this regular pattern of comparison. You must use an entirely different word for the comparative and the superlative.

This wine is *bad.* (positive)
This wine is *worse.* (comparative)
not "badder"

This wine is *the worst.* (superlative)
not "baddest"

**In Latin:** Comparison of adjectives have the same three degrees as in English: positive, comparative and superlative. In all three degrees, adjectives are declined through the various cases according to their declension. Remember that, like all adjectives, they must agree with their noun in case, gender and number (see **What is a Descriptive Adjective?**, p. 131).

1. The positive degree of the adjective is simply the vocabulary or dictionary form of the adjective.

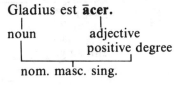

   Gladius est **ācer.**
   noun — adjective, positive degree
   nom. masc. sing.

   *The sword is **sharp**.*

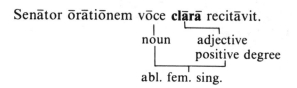

Senātor ōrātiōnem vōce **clārā** recitāvit.

noun — adjective, positive degree

abl. fem. sing.

*The senator recited the speech in a* ***clear*** *voice.*

2. The comparative degree is formed with the GENITIVE MASCULINE SINGULAR STEM of the adjective in the positive degree + *-IOR* (for the masculine and feminine) OR *-IUS* (for the neuter). These comparative adjectives are declined like the two-form adjectives in Group B (see p. 134) in the third declension. See your textbook for the complete declension.

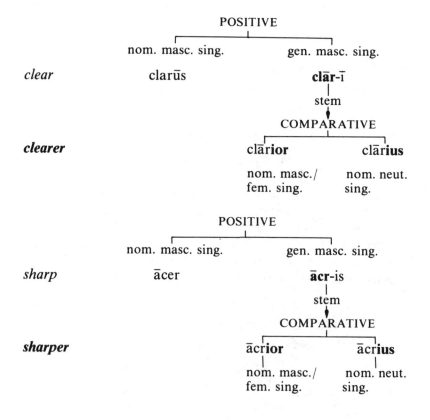

POSITIVE

| | nom. masc. sing. | gen. masc. sing. |
|---|---|---|
| *clear* | clarūs | **clār**-ī |

stem → COMPARATIVE

| | | |
|---|---|---|
| ***clearer*** | clār**ior** | clār**ius** |
| | nom. masc./ fem. sing. | nom. neut. sing. |

POSITIVE

| | nom. masc. sing. | gen. masc. sing. |
|---|---|---|
| *sharp* | ācer | **ācr**-is |

stem → COMPARATIVE

| | | |
|---|---|---|
| ***sharper*** | ācr**ior** | ācr**ius** |
| | nom. masc./ fem. sing. | nom. neut. sing. |

Hic discipulus respōnsum **clārius** dedit.

noun — adjective, comparative degree

acc. neut. sing.

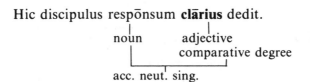

*This student gave a* ***clearer*** *answer.*

Lingua est **ācrior** quam gladius.

noun — adjective, comparative degree

nom. fem. sing.

*The tongue is* ***sharper*** *than the sword.*

- Some adjectives form their comparative degree with **magis** (*more*) placed before the adjective in the positive degree. This procedure is regular with adjectives whose ending is preceded by a vowel (for example, **dubius**, **dubia**, **dubium**).

Victōria nunc vidētur **magis dubia.**

noun — adjective, comparative degree

nom. fem. sing.

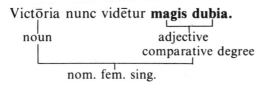

*Victory now seems* ***more doubtful.***

3. The superlative degree is formed with the GENITIVE MASCULINE SINGULAR STEM of the adjective in the positive degree + *-ISSIMUS, —A, —UM.* These superlative adjectives are declined like **bonus, -a, -um** in Group A (see p. 133)

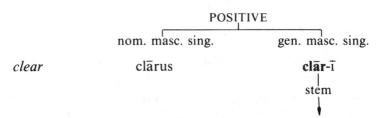

POSITIVE

| | nom. masc. sing. | gen. masc. sing. |
|---|---|---|
| *clear* | clārus | **clār**-ī |

stem
↓

SUPERLATIVE

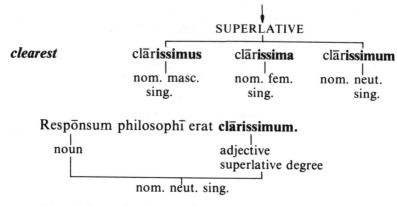

| | | | |
|---|---|---|---|
| ***clearest*** | clā**rissimus** | clā**rissima** | clā**rissimum** |
| | nom. masc. sing. | nom. fem. sing. | nom. neut. sing. |

Respōnsum philosophī erat **clārissimum.**

noun — adjective, superlative degree

nom. neut. sing.

*The philosopher's answer was* ***most (very) clear.***

However, when the adjective ends in **-er**, the superlative degree is formed with the NOMINATIVE MASCULINE SINGULAR + *-RIMUS, -A, -UM.* These superlative adjectives belong to Group A (see p. 133).

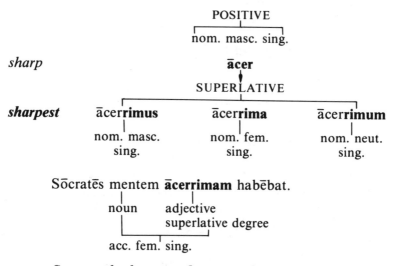

POSITIVE

nom. masc. sing.

*sharp* **ācer**

SUPERLATIVE

| | | | |
|---|---|---|---|
| ***sharpest*** | ācer**rimus** | ācer**rima** | ācer**rimum** |
| | nom. masc. sing. | nom. fem. sing. | nom. neut. sing. |

Sōcratēs mentem **ācerrimam** habēbat.

noun — adjective, superlative degree

acc. fem. sing.

*Socrates had a* ***very sharp*** *mind.*

- Some adjectives form the superlative degree with **maximē** (*most, very*) placed before the adjective in the positive degree. This procedure is regular with adjectives whose ending is preceded by a vowel. These adjectives belong to Group A (see p. 133).

Victōria nunc vidētur **maximē dubia.**

noun — adjective superlative degree

nom. fem. sing.

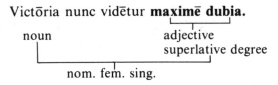

*Victory now seems **most doubtful.***

Consult your textbook for the few adjectives which form their superlative in other ways.

Below is a chart which summarizes the formation of the comparative and superlative degree of the adjectives.

| Positive degree | Comparative degree | Superlative degree |
|---|---|---|
| ↓ | Stem: genitive masculine singular of positive degree + **-ior** for masc. & fem. + **-ius** for neut. ↓ | Stem: genitive masculine singular of positive degree + **-issimus, -a, -um** or Stem: nominative masculine singular of positive degree + **-rimus, -a, -um** ↓ |
| clār**us, -a, -um** genitive stem: **clār-** | clār**ior**, clār**ius** | clār**issimus, -a, -um** |
| ā**cer**, ācr**is**, ācr**e** genitive stem: **ācr-** | ācr**ior**, ācr**ius** | ācer**rimus, -a, -um** |
| | Group B: 3rd declension | Group A: 1st/2nd declension |

Just as in English, in Latin there are several irregular comparisons of adjectives that are used frequently. These must be memorized, but since words used in English are derived directly from the Latin, the task should not be difficult.

| Positive | Comparative | English derivative | Superlative | English derivative |
|---|---|---|---|---|
| (masculine) | (masculine) | | (masculine) | |
| bonus<br>*good* | melior<br>*better* | ameliorate | optimus | optimist<br>*best* |
| malus<br>*bad* | pēior<br>*worse* | pejorative | pessimus<br>*worst* | pessimist |
| magnus<br>*great* | maior<br>*greater* | major | maximus<br>*greatest* | maximum |

Consult your textbook for the other few, but important, adjectives that have an irregular comparison.

## What is a Possessive Adjective?

A POSSESSIVE ADJECTIVE is a word which describes a noun by showing who possesses it.

**In English:** Here is a list of the possessive adjectives:

| Person | Singular | Plural |
|---|---|---|
| 1st | my | our |
| 2nd | your | your |
| 3rd | his, her, its | their |

The possessive adjective refers only to the person who possesses, the possessor.

Aeneas was Venus' son. Aeneas was *her* son.
possessor

Aeneas' mother was a goddess. *His* mother was a goddess.
possessor

Troy's walls were high. *Its* walls were high.
possessor

When the 3rd person singular (*his, her, its*) and plural (*their*) are used, two meanings are often possible. For example, the sentence "Medea murdered her children" could mean that Medea murdered her own children or someone else's. Usually the context of the sentence helps us understand the correct meaning; however, when there is the possibility of a misunderstanding, the word *own* is added after the possessive adjective: "Medea murdered her own children." In this case, and whenever *own* can be added after the possessive adjective, the possessive adjective is called **REFLEXIVE**; it "reflects back" to the possessor which is the subject of the sentence or clause.

The goddess saw *her* father. [Referring to her own father.]
subject reflexive

If the possessive adjective refers to a possessor other than the subject of the sentence or clause, it is called **NON-REFLEXIVE**.

The goddess saw *her* father. [Referring to the girl's father.]
non-reflexive

**In Latin:** The possessive adjective refers to the person who possesses, the possessor, and the ending of the possessive adjective agrees in case, gender and number with the noun possessed.

Aeneas was Venus' son. Aeneas was *her* son.
noun possessed

Aeneas' mother was a goddess. *His* mother was a goddess.
noun possessed

Troy's walls were high. *Its* walls were high.
noun possessed

The Latin possessive adjectives **meus, -a, -um** (*my*), etc. belong to Group A, see p. 133. The third person singular and plural (**suus, -a, -um**) can only have one meaning, *his own, her own, its own* and *their own,* i.e. reflexive.

Here are the steps you should follow to choose the correct possessive adjective and its proper form:

1. Indicate the possessor with the stem of possessive adjective

| | |
|---|---|
| *my* | me- |
| *your (sing.)* | tu- |
| *his, her, its (own)* | su- |
| *our* | nost- (nostr-)[1] |
| *your (pl.)* | vest- (vestr-)[1] |
| *their (own)* | su- |

2. Identify the case, gender and number of the noun possessed.

- *Aeneas loved* ***his*** *mother.*
  Aenēas mātrem su ? amābat.

  Case: Direct object = accusative
  Aeneas loved *whom?* His mother.
  Gender: **Mātrem** (nominative, **māter**) is feminine.
  Number: Singular

[1]Consult your textbook to see if you should use **nost-** or **nostr-** (**vest-** or **vestr-**) as the stem.

- *Venus often gave comfort to **her** son.*
  Venus fīliō su ? consōlātiōnem saepe dedit.

  Case: Indirect object = dative
  Venus gave comfort *to whom?* To her son.
  Gender: **Fīliō** (nominative, **fīlius**) is masculine.
  Number: Singular

- *Citizens, the walls of **your** city are not high enough!*
  Cīvēs, moenia urbis vestr ? nōn sunt satis alta.

  Case: Possessive = genitive
  *Whose* walls are not high enough? Your city's.
  Gender: **Urbis** (nominative, **urbs**) is feminine.
  Number: Singular

3. Provide the ending which reflects the case, gender and number of the noun possessed.

- *Aeneas loved **his** mother.*
  Aenēas mātrem **suam** amābat.

  noun — possessive adjective
  acc. fem. sing.

- *Venus often gave comfort to **her** son.*
  Venus fīliō **suō** consōlātiōnem saepe dedit.

  noun — possessive adjective
  dat. masc. sing.

- *Citizens, the walls of **your** city are not high enough!*
  Cīvēs, moenia urbis **vestrae** nōn sunt satis alta.

  noun — possessive adjective
  gen. fem. sing.

It is very important to determine the possessor in the case of *his, her, its* and *their*. In English, these possessive adjectives can be reflexive or non-reflexive. In Latin the third person possessive adjective **suus, -a, -um** is reflexive. For the non-reflexive Latin uses the genitives of the personal pronoun **is, ea, id: eius, eōrum** and **eārum** (see p. 46).

| | Literally | English translation |
|---|---|---|
| eius | *of him* | his |
| | *of her* | her |
| | *of it* | its |
| eōrum | *of them* | their (masculine & neuter) |
| eārum | *of them* | their (feminine) |

Since these forms are always in the genitive case, the endings of these substitutes for the possessive adjective do not change to agree with the case of the noun possessed. The endings change, however, to reflect the gender and number of the plural possessor.

*The goddess saw* ***her*** *father.* [Referring to the girl's father.]
Dea patrem **eius** vīdit.

personal pronoun
gen. fem. sing.
referring to *the girl*

Compare this sentence with the one below where the possessive adjective is used.

*The goddess saw* ***her*** *father.* [Referring to her own father.]
Dea patrem **suum** vīdit.

reflexive possessive adjective
acc. masc. sing.
agrees with **patrem** (*father*)

Possessive adjectives are frequently omitted in Latin if there is no doubt as to who is the possessor and if there is no reason to emphasize the adjectives. However, they are usually added in the English when one translates.

Eurōpa cum amīcis lūdit.
*Europa is playing with* ***her*** *friends.*

## What is an Interrogative Adjective?

An **INTERROGATIVE ADJECTIVE** is a word which asks a question about a noun.

**In English:** There are three interrogative adjectives, ***what*** and ***which*** and ***whose.***

*What* book is on the table?[1]
noun

*Which* person is in the room?
noun

*Whose* book is on the table?[2]
noun

The words *what* and *which* are used interchangeably to ask for a variety of information about a noun. For instance, they can ask

1. the name of a person or thing

   *What* goddess did Niobe offend? The goddess Latona.
   *Which* city was conquered? The city of Troy.

2. the nature or kind of person or thing

   *What (sort of)* woman offended the goddess? A proud woman.

3. the amount or degree of something

   With *what* sorrow did the mother bewail her dead children? With the greatest sorrow.

---

[1]Do not confuse with "*What* is on the table?" where *what* is a pronoun. See p. 161.
[2]The possessive *whose* as in "*Whose* book is on the table?" will be discussed under interrogative pronouns, since Latin considers *whose* a pronoun.

**In Latin:** There are four interrogative adjectives and the one you choose will depend on the type of information being asked about the noun. As in English, the interrogative adjective stands before the noun it modifies. As you will see below, Latin sometimes uses an interrogative pronoun as an interrogative adjective. Remember that all interrogative adjectives, as well as pronoun forms used as adjectives, must follow the rules of agreement of all adjectives: they agree with the noun they modify in case, gender and number.

1. the name of a person or thing

   When *what* or *which* is used in the sense of "what is the name of...," Latin uses the interrogative pronoun **quis** as an interrogative adjective. Consult your Latin textbook for the complete declension.

   ***What** woman offended the goddess? Niobe.*
   **Quis** mulier deam offendit? Niobē.
   interr. adj. — noun
   nom. fem. sing.

   ***Which** army was conquered? The Trojan army.*
   **Quis** exercitus victus est? Exercitus Trōiānus.
   interr. adj. — noun
   nom. masc. sing.

2. the nature or kind of person or thing

   When *what* or *which* is used in the sense of "what kind of...," Latin uses either one of two interrogative adjectives.

   - **quī, quae, quod** declined in all the cases as the relative pronoun. Consult your textbook for the complete declension.

*What woman offended the goddess? A proud woman.*
**Quae** mulier deam offendit? Mulier superba.

interr. adj. — noun
nom. fem. sing.

- **quālis, quāle** declined as an adjective of the third declension (see chart, Group B, p. 134).

*With **what** punishment did the goddess inflict her? With a severe punishment.*
**Quālī** poenā dea eam affēcit? Poenā sevērā.

interr. adj. — noun
abl. fem. sing.

3. the amount or degree of something

When *what* or *which* is used in the sense of "how much . . . " or "to what degree . . . ," Latin uses the interrogative adjective **quantus, quanta, quantum** declined as an adjective of Group A. Consult your textbook for the complete declension.

- *With **what** sorrow did the mother bewail the dead children? With the greatest sorrow.*
**Quantō** dolore māter puerōs mortuōs flēbat? Maximō dolōre.

interr. adj. — noun
abl. masc. sing.

4. the quantity of something or the number of persons

When you ask the question "how many," Latin uses the interrogative adjective **quot.** It is not declined; the same form is used in all cases.

- ***How many*** *arrows did Apollo shoot? Seven arrows.*
  **Quot** sagittās Apollo coniēcit? Septem sagittās.

  interr. adj. — noun
  acc. fem. pl.

## What is a Demonstrative Adjective?

A DEMONSTRATIVE ADJECTIVE is a word used to point out a noun. It is called demonstrative because it points out a person or thing. The word demonstrative comes from the Latin **dēmonstrāre** meaning *to point out* or *show.*

**In English:** The demonstrative adjectives are ***this*** and ***that*** in the singular and ***these*** and ***those*** in the plural. They are a rare example of English adjectives agreeing with the noun they modify: *this* changes to *these* before a plural noun and *that* changes to *those.*

| | |
|---|---|
| *this* arrow | *these* arrows |
| *that* book | *those* books |

The distinction between *this* and *that* can be used to contrast one object with another, or to refer to things that are not the same distance away. We generally say *this* (or *these*) for the closer object, and *that* (or *those*) for the one farther away.

Cupid has two arrows. *This* arrow is sharp,
showing contrast

causing love.

*That* arrow is dull, causing love to flee.[1]
|
showing contrast

"*These* arrows are my weapons," says Cupid. "I do
|
referring to
arrows at hand

not use *those* weapons."
|
referring to
rocks at a distance

**In Latin:** There are four types of demonstrative adjectives: each type reflects the relationship of the speaker to the object or person pointed out (see below). Each type is declined in the masculine, feminine and neuter, singular and plural. Since demonstrative adjectives have endings in some of the cases different from the descriptive adjectives, you must use special care in learning them. Consult your textbook for the complete declension. Once you have identified which of the four types to use, remember that, being an adjective, the demonstrative adjective must agree with its noun in case, gender and number. To choose the correct form, follow the steps on p. 136.

In each pronoun the first form is masculine, the second feminine, the third neuter.

1. **Hic, haec, hoc**—the demonstrative adjective to point out a noun near or belonging to the writer or speaker.

   • **Hoc** consilium est optimum.
   demon. adj. — noun
   nom. neut. sing.

   ***This** plan **(of mine)** is the best.*

---

[1]Cupid shot Apollo with his sharp arrow, causing the god to fall in love. The dull arrow shot into Daphne caused her to flee. Just as Apollo was about to overtake the maiden she was changed into a laurel, which Apollo made his sacred tree.

- Lege **hōs** librōs!

  demon. adj. — noun
  acc. masc. pl.

  *Read **these** books **(which I have here)**!*

2. **Ille, illa, illud**—the demonstrative adjective to point out a noun away from the speaker or writer and the person spoken to.

   - Cicerō, **ille** senātor nihil dīcit!

     demon. adj. — noun
     nom. masc. sing.

     *Cicero, **that** senator **(over there)** is saying nothing.*

   - Glōriam **illārum** fēminārum memoriā semper tenēbimus.

     demon. adj. — noun
     gen. fem. pl.

     *We shall always remember the fame of **those** women.*

3. **Iste, ista, istud**—the demonstrative adjective to point out a noun near or belonging to the person spoken to.

   - **Ista** fābula est mihi grāta.

     demon. adj. — noun
     nom. fem. sing.

     ***That** story **(of yours)** is pleasing to me.*

   - Dabō **istīs** līberīs dōna.

     demon. adj. — noun
     dat. masc. pl.

     *I shall give gifts to **those** children **(of yours)**.*

4. **Is, ea, id**—the demonstrative adjective merely to point out a noun already mentioned or to be mentioned. There is little

reference to the speaker or writer, to the person spoken to or spoken about. It is a weak demonstrative adjective and at times can be translated by the English indefinite article.

- **Eō** tempore Caesar Gallōs superābat.

demon. adj. — noun
abl. neut. sing.

*At **that** time Caesar was overcoming the Gauls.*

- Desīderant **eum** ducem quī agere nōn dubitet.

demon. adj. — noun
acc. masc. sing.

*They desire a **(that)** leader who will not hesitate to act.*

In addition to pointing out a person or thing, each Latin demonstrative adjective has other functions. For example, the demonstrative adjective frequently serves as a personal pronoun (see **What is a Personal Pronoun?**, p. 40). Consult your textbook for other special uses of each demonstrative adjective.

## What is an Adverb?

An ADVERB is a word that modifies (describes) a verb, an adjective or another adverb. Adverbs indicate quantity, time, place, intensity and manner. They tell how much, when, where, to what extent, and how.

Theseus fights *well.*
verb adverb

The labyrinth was *very* complicated.
adverb adjective

Ariadne fell in love *too easily.*
adverb adverb

**In English:** Listed below are some examples of adverbs.

- of quantity or degree

  Theseus feared ***little.***
  The plan of escape worked ***very well.***

  These adverbs answer the question *how much* or *how well.*

- of time

  Theseus will come ***soon.***
  The ship arrived ***late.***

  These adverbs answer the question *when.*

- of place

  The Minotaur looked ***around.***
  The other youths were left ***behind.***

These adverbs answer the question *where.*

- of intensity

  The Minotaur did not ***actually*** eat the youths.
  Theseus ***really*** killed the Minotaur.

  These adverbs are used for emphasis.

- of manner

  Theseus escaped ***cleverly.***
  Ariadne planned the escape ***carefully.***

  These adverbs answer the question *how.* They are very common adverbs and can usually be recognized by their *-ly* ending.

Some, though not many, adverbs in English are identical in form to the corresponding adjectives:

| | |
|---|---|
| Theseus ran *fast.* (adverb) | Theseus escaped in a *fast* ship. (adjective) |

**In Latin:** There are two general endings which can be added to adjective stems to indicate adverbs: **-iter** and **-e.** In addition, however, there are many adverbs which you must learn independently of any adjective. Compare the following:

| Adverb | Adjective |
|---|---|
| Theseus **celeriter** cucurrit.<br>*Theseus ran **fast.*** | Theseus nāve **celerī** effūgit.<br>*Theseus escaped in a **fast** ship.* |

Although the adverb and adjective are obviously related, they cannot be used interchangeably, for adverbs use the adverb endings of **-iter** or **-e**, while adjectives agree in case, gender and number with the nouns they modify.

Just like adjectives, adverbs can have degrees: positive, comparative and superlative. The meaning and the formation of these degrees of adverbs are very similar to the meaning and the formation of the degrees of adjectives (see **What is Meant by Comparison of Adjectives?**, p. 140). Consult your Latin textbook for the formation of the comparative and superlative degrees of adverbs.

The most common adverbs have irregular comparisons similar to that of the adjectives which have irregular comparisons.

| | | | |
|---|---|---|---|
| Adjective: | bonus, -a, -um<br>*good* | melior, melius<br>*better* | optimus, -a, -um<br>*best* |
| Adverb: | bene<br>*well* | melius<br>*better, rather well* | optimē<br>*very well* |

These irregularly compared adverbs must be memorized for they are very important.

N.B.: Adverbs are always invariable (never change ending), whereas adjectives must always agree with the word they modify in case, gender and number.

## What is an Interrogative Pronoun?

An **INTERROGATIVE PRONOUN** is a pronoun (a word used in place of a noun) which introduces a question; *interrogative* is related to *interrogate,* meaning *to question.*

**In English:** Different interrogative pronouns are used for asking about persons and for asking about things.

| | |
|---|---|
| *What* is on the table?[1] | refers to a thing |
| *Who* is in the room? | refers to a person |

The personal interrogative pronoun, like some of the personal pronouns in English, has different case forms. (See **What is a Personal Pronoun?**, p. 40.)

- ***Who*** is the nominative form and is used for the subject of the sentence.

  *Who* wrote that book?
  subject — direct object

  *Who* will help you?
  subject — direct object

- ***Whom*** is the objective form and is used for the direct object of the sentence and, in standard written English, for the object of a preposition (see **What are Objects?**, p. 31).

  *Whom* do you know here?
  direct object — subject

[1]Do not confuse with "*What book* is on the table?" where *what* is an interrogative adjective. See p. 151.

From *whom* did you get the book?

object of preposition *from* (*whom*) — subject (*you*)

In spoken or colloquial English you will often hear *who* used incorrectly for *whom* in the objective case. In colloquial English the two sentences above could be expressed as follows:

*Who* do you know here?

direct object (*Who*)

*Who* did you get the book from?

object of preposition *from* (*Who*)

Whether the standard *whom* is used or the informal *who,* the function of the interrogative pronoun remains the same. It is important that you be able to distinguish *who* in the nominative form and *who* used as a substitute for *whom* in the objective form.

- ***Whose*** is the possessive form and is used to ask about possession or ownership.

I found a stylus.[1] *Whose* is it?
I have Mary's book. *Whose* do you have?

The interrogative pronoun which is used to ask about things does not have case forms: ***what*** is used regardless of its function in the sentence.

*What* is in the chest?

subject (*What*)

---

[1]The Romans wrote with the pointed end of a little stick, called a stylus, making an impression on a wax tablet.

*What* are you doing?
direct object

As you can see from all the examples above, *who* and *what* are considered singular, and when they are the subject of the sentence, they have a singular verb. The answer can be in the singular or plural.

- Who *is coming* tonight? (singular verb) — Mark *is coming* tonight. (singular verb)

  or

  Mark and Julia *are coming* tonight. (plural verb)

- What *is* in the chest? (singular verb) — The treasure *is* in the chest. (singular verb)

  or

  The treasures *are* in the chest. (plural verb)

Similarly, *who(m)* and *whose* can refer to one or more persons. Since these forms can never be the subject of the sentence, they do not affect the verb of the sentence. The answer, however, can be in the singular or plural.

- *Who(m)* is the soldier killing? — He is killing *a warrior.* (singular)

  or

  He is killing *many warriors.* (plural)

- *Whose* are these weapons?[1] They are the *soldier's*.
  (singular)

  or

  They are the *soldiers'*.
  (plural)

**In Latin:** As in English, different interrogative pronouns are used for asking about persons and for asking about things (**quis, quid**). Let us first look at the interrogative pronoun referring to persons.

The personal interrogative pronoun is fully declined in all cases. Unlike English interrogative pronouns which make no distinction in gender and number, Latin has a plural form for each case. Some cases even make a gender distinction and have a different form for the masculine plural and the feminine plural. The person asking the question, the questioner, can use the plural form of the interrogative pronoun if a plural answer is expected. The questioner can also choose a feminine plural form if reference is being made to a group of women.

To find the correct form of the interrogative pronoun, here is a series of steps to follow:

1. Determine the function of the interrogative pronoun in the question to establish the case.

| | | | |
|---|---|---|---|
| • Is it the subject of the question? | (Who?) | ⟶ | Nominative |
| • Does it show possession? | (Whose?) | ⟶ | Genitive |
| • Is it the indirect object of the verb? | (To or for whom?) | ⟶ | Dative |

[1]In English *whose* in this sentence is a pronoun; the same question could be asked, "*Whose* weapons are these?" where the *whose* is an adjective modifying the noun *weapons*. In Latin only the pronoun is used for *whose* with the meaning expanded into the literal "of whom" (see p. 166).

| | | |
|---|---|---|
| • Is it the direct object of the verb? | (Whom?) → | Accusative |
| • Is it the object of a preposition? Does the preposition take the accusative or the ablative as its object? | (With whom?) → (Through whom?) | Ablative or Accusative |

2. If the context indicates that the questioner is expecting a singular answer, choose the form of the interrogative pronoun which corresponds to the case established under step 1 above. There is no gender distinction in the singular.

3. If the context indicates that the questioner is expecting a plural answer, one of the plural forms of the interrogative pronoun is used.

   When there is a masculine and feminine plural form:

   - choose the masculine plural when referring to a group of all men or to a mixed group of men and women.
   - choose the feminine plural when referring to a group of women only.

Here are a few examples. Since there is no way of knowing if the English interrogative pronoun is singular, masculine plural or feminine plural when a question is out of context, context is provided between brackets for each question below.

- ***who*** (subject) = nominative **quis** (sing.)
  **quī** (masc. pl.) **quae** (fem. pl.)

***Who** is in the dining room?* [Singular answer expected; i.e. only one person in dining room.]

Function of *who*: subject
Case: nominative
Number: singular

**Quis** est in trīclīniō?
|
nom. sing.

***Who** is coming today?*

[Plural answer expected; i.e. group of people coming.]

Function of *who*: subject
Case: nominative
Gender and Number: masculine plural

**Quī** hodiē veniunt?
nom. masc. pl.

**Quae** hodiē veniunt?
nom. fem. pl.

[Plural answer expected; i.e. group of women coming.]

- ***whose*** (possessive) = genitive **cuius** (masc. and fem. sing.)
  **quōrum** (masc. pl.) **quārum** (fem. pl.)

*I have his book. **Whose** do you have?*

[Singular answer expected; masculine or feminine.]

Function of *whose*: possessive
Case: genitive
Number: singular

Librum eius habeō. **Cuius** habēs?
gen. sing.

*The victors are gathering weapons.*
***Whose** are they gathering?*

[The men's.]

Function of *whose*: possessive
Case: genitive
Gender and number: masculine plural

Victōrēs arma colligunt. **Quōrum** colligunt?
gen. pl. masc.

*I see jewels in the chest.* ***Whose*** *are they?* [The women's.]

Function of *whose*: possessive
Case: genitive
Gender and number: feminine plural

Gemmās in arcā videō. **Quārum** sunt?
gen. pl. fem.

Even if in English the questions above were asked with the *whose* as an adjective: "*Whose* book do you have?" Latin would still use the pronoun for *whose*. The literal translation would be "The book *of whom* do you have?" There is no possessive interrogative adjective in Latin, only the possessive interrogative pronoun (see p. 151 fn. 2 and p. 164 fn. 1).

- ***who(m)*** (direct object) = accusative **quem** (sing.)
  **quōs** (masc. pl.) **quās** (fem. pl.)

The interrogative pronoun used as an object is more difficult to identify because *whom,* which is the standard form, has been replaced by *who* in colloquial language. You will, therefore, have to analyze the sentence carefully to find the grammatical function of *who(m).*

***Who(m)*** *do you see?* [Singular answer expected.]

Function of *who*: direct object of *see*
*You* is the subject of *see.*
Case: **Vidēre** (*to see*) requires an accusative object.
Number: singular

**Quem** vidēs?
acc. sing.

***Who(m)*** *is the soldier killing?* [Referring to many men being killed.]

Function of *who:* direct object of *is killing*
*Soldier* is the subject of *is killing.*
Case: **Necāre** (*to kill*) requires an accusative object.
Gender and Number: masculine plural

**Quōs** mīles necat?
acc. masc. pl.

***Who(m)*** *are the children seeking?* [Referring to their mothers.]

Function of *who:* direct object of *are seeking*
*Children* is the subject of *are seeking.*
Case: **Quaerere** (*to seek*) requires an accusative object.
Gender and number: feminine plural

**Quās** līberī quaerunt?
acc. fem. pl.

***Who(m)*** *can I believe?* [Singular answer expected.]

Function of *who:* object of *can believe*
*I* is the subject of *can believe.*
Case: **Crēdere** (*to believe*) requires a dative object.
Number: singular

**Cuī** crēdere possum?
dat. sing.

- ***who(m)*** (indirect object) = dative **cuī** (sing.)
  **quibus** (pl.)

***Who*** *shall I send the letter to?*[1] [Singular answer expected.]

| *Who* shall I send the letter *to*? | ——→ | *To whom* shall I send the letter? |
|---|---|---|

Function of *who:* indirect object of *shall send*
*I* is the subject of *shall send.*
*Letter* is the direct object.
Case: dative
Number: singular

[1]Remember to restructure the dangling preposition, see p. 193.

**Cuī** litterās mittam?
dat. sing.

***Who are you working for?*** [Plural answer expected.]

| *Who* are you working *for?* ——→ *For whom* are you working? |
|---|

Function of *who:* indirect object of *are working*
*You* is the subject of *are working.*
Case: dative
Number: plural

**Quibus** labōrātis?
dat. pl.

- ***who(m)*** (object of preposition) =

| | |
|---|---|
| accusative preposition | + **quem** (sing.) |
| | + **quōs** (masc. pl.) |
| | + **quās** (fem. pl.) |
| ablative preposition | + **quō** (sing.) |
| | + **quibus** (pl.) |

***Who(m) are you fighting against?*** [Singular answer expected.]

| *Who* are you fighting *against?* ——→ *Against whom* are you fighting? |
|---|

Function of *who:* object of preposition *against*
Case: **Contrā** (*against*) requires the accusative case.
Number: singular

Contrā **quem** pugnās?
acc. sing.

Contrā **quōs** pugnās? [Plural answer expected; you are fighting against many men.]
acc. masc. pl.

Contrā **quās** pugnās? [Plural answer expected; you are fighting against many women.]
acc. fem. pl.

***Who(m) is he talking about?*** [Singular answer expected.]

| *Who* is he talking *about*? —▸ *About whom* is he talking? |
|---|

Function of *who:* object of preposition *about*
Case: **Dē** (*about*) requires the ablative case.
Number: singular

Dē **quō** loquitur?
abl. sing.

***Who(m) are you coming with?*** [Plural answer expected.]

| *Who* are you coming *with*?—▸ *With whom* are you coming? |
|---|

Function of *who:* object of preposition *with*
Case: **Cum** (*with*) requires the ablative case.
Number: plural

Cum **quibus** (or **quibuscum**) venīs?
abl. pl.

Cum **quō** (or **quōcum**) venīs? [Singular answer expected.]
abl. sing.

Now let us look at the interrogative pronoun referring to things, in neuter gender. The same system of cases applies as for interrogative pronouns referring to persons, but there are fewer forms; there is only one gender—neuter. Often the same form is used for two cases: *What* (**quid**) is both nominative and accusative.

To find the correct form of the interrogative pronoun, follow these two steps:

1. Determine the function of *what* in the question to establish the case.
2. If the context indicates that the questioner is expecting a singular answer, choose the singular form; if a plural answer is expected, choose the plural form.

Here are a few examples:

***What*** *is in the chest?* [Singular answer expected.]
subject

**Quid** est in arcā?
nominative singular

***What*** *are you doing?*
direct object

**Quid** facis?
accusative singular

***What*** *do you see in the city?* [Plural answer expected.]
direct object

**Quae** in urbe vidēs?
accusative plural

## What is a Possessive Pronoun?

A **POSSESSIVE PRONOUN** is a word which replaces a noun and which also shows who possesses that noun.

Whose house is that? *Mine.*

*Mine* is a pronoun which replaces the noun *house* and which shows who possesses that noun.

**In English:** Possessive pronouns refer only to the person who possesses, not to the object possessed.

Example 1. Is that your house? Yes, it is *mine.*
Example 2. Are those your books? Yes, they are *mine.*

The same possessive pronoun *mine* is used, although the object possessed is singular in Example 1 (*house*) and plural in Example 2 (*books*).

Here is a list of the English possessive pronouns:

| | |
|---|---|
| mine | ours |
| yours | yours |
| his, hers, its | theirs |

**In Latin:** To express the possessive pronoun Latin uses the possessive adjective (see **What is a Possessive Adjective?**, p. 146). To choose the correct form, follow the same steps as for the possessive adjective (see p. 148). When it is an adjective, the noun it modifies is stated; when it is a pronoun, the noun is not stated, but understood.

- Estne illa domus tua? Ita, est **mea.** [domus]
  (mea … domus: nom. fem. sing.)

*Is that your house? Yes it is* **mine.** [*my house*]

- Suntne illī librī tuī? Ita, sunt **meī.** [librī]
  nom. masc. pl.

  *Are those your books? Yes they are **mine.*** [*my books*]

## What is a Reflexive Pronoun?

A **REFLEXIVE PRONOUN** is a pronoun which is used either as the object of a verb or as the object of a preposition, and which refers back to the subject of the sentence: it *reflects* back to the subject.

**In English:** Reflexive pronouns end with *-self* in the singular and *-selves* in the plural:

| Person | Singular | Plural |
|---|---|---|
| 1st | myself | ourselves |
| 2nd | yourself | yourselves |
| 3rd | himself<br>herself<br>itself | themselves |

Observe their usage:

1. as object of a verb

- I cut *myself* with my sword.
  subject — direct object

  *I* is subject of *cut; myself* (same person) is the direct object.

- You should write *yourself* a note.

  subject — indirect object

  *You* is the subject of *should write; yourself* (same person) is indirect object.

2. as object of a preposition

- He thinks only of *himself.*

  subject — object of preposition

  *He* is the subject of *thinks; himself* (same person) is object of the preposition *of.*

- You talk about *yourself* too much.

  subject — object of preposition

  *You* is the subject of *thinks; yourself* (same person) is object of the preposition *about.*

**In Latin:** As in English there are reflexive pronouns for each of the different personal pronouns (1st, 2nd, and 3rd persons).

| Subject Pronouns Nominative | Reflexive Pronouns Genitive | Dative | Accusative | Ablative | |
|---|---|---|---|---|---|
| | | | Singular | | |
| 1 ego | meī | mihi | mē | mē | *myself* |
| 2 tū | tuī | tibi | tē | tē | *yourself* |
| 3 is<br>ea<br>id | suī | sibi | sē | sē | *himself*<br>*herself*<br>*itself* |
| | | | Plural | | |
| 1 nōs | nostrī | nōbīs | nōs | nōbīs | *ourselves* |
| 2 vōs | vestrī | vōbīs | vōs | vōbīs | *yourselves* |
| 3 eī<br>eae<br>ea | suī | sibi | sē | sē | *themselves* |

If you compare this table with that of the personal pronouns (see p. 46), you will find that the pronouns differ in the third person, singular and plural.

Like English reflexive pronouns, Latin reflexive pronouns are used as objects of verbs, as indirect objects and as objects of prepositions, and as objective genitives (see p. 30).

1. as object of a verb

- **Mē** gladiō meō secuī.

  reflexive pronoun
  direct object = accusative

  *I cut **myself** with my sword.*

2. as indirect object

- Annotātiōnem **tibi** scrībere dēbēs.

  reflexive pronoun
  indirect object = dative

  *You ought to write **yourself** a note.*

3. as object of preposition

- Contrā **sē** pugnāvit.

  reflexive pronoun
  object of preposition **contrā** = accusative

  *He fought against **himself**.*

4. as objective genitive (see p. 30)

- Omnis natūra est servātrix **suī.**

  reflexive pronoun
  objective genitive (*the protector of itself*)

  *All nature is the protector of* ***itself.***

## What is a Demonstrative Pronoun?

A DEMONSTRATIVE PRONOUN replaces a noun which has been mentioned before. It is called demonstrative because it points out a person or thing. The word demonstrative comes from the Latin **demonstrare** meaning *to point out* or *show,* which also gives the English word *demonstrate.*

**In English:** The demonstrative pronouns are ***this*** and ***that*** in the singular (meaning *this one* and *that one*) and ***these*** and ***those*** in the plural.

The distinction between *this* and *that* can be used to contrast one object with another, or to refer to things that are not the same distance away. We use *this* or *these* for the closer object, and *that* or *those* for the one farther away.

Cupid has two arrows. *This* (one) is sharp; *that* (one) is dull. Cupid shoots *this* (one) into Apollo; he shoots *that* (one) into Daphne.[1]

"*These* are my weapons," says Cupid. "I do not use *those*."

*These*: referring to the arrows at hand

*those*: referring to rocks at a distance

[1]See fn. 1, p. 155.

**In Latin:** Complete declensions of the demonstrative pronouns **hic, haec, hoc** (*this*) and **ille, illa, illud** (*that*) are given in your textbook in all cases, singular and plural. The forms are the same as those of the demonstrative adjective (see **What is a Demonstrative Adjective?**, p. 154), but obviously instead of modifying a noun, the pronoun replaces the noun.

The form of the demonstrative pronoun depends on a series of factors: the case is determined by the function of the pronoun in the sentence or clause; the gender is determined by the gender of the noun the pronoun replaces (the antecedent); the number is determined by the idea being expressed.

To find the correct form of the demonstrative pronoun, here are a series of steps to follow:

1. Determine the function, and therefore the case, of the demonstrative pronoun in the sentence or clause.

   - Is it the subject? → nominative
   - Is it the direct object? → accusative
   - Is it an indirect object? → dative
   - Is it the object of a preposition? → accusative or ablative
   - Is it the possessive modifier? → genitive

2. Determine the gender of the antecedent.

   - Is it masculine, feminine, or neuter?

3. Determine the number of the idea being expressed.

   - If the idea is *this (one)* or *that (one)*, choose the singular form.
   - If the idea is *these* or *those,* choose the plural form.

4. Select the proper form of the demonstrative pronoun based on steps 1-3.

Here are a series of examples to illustrate these steps.

- *Cupid has two arrows.* ***This (one)*** *is sharp;* ***that (one)*** *is dull.*

1. Case: *This (one)* = subject = nominative
   *that (one)* = subject = nominative
2. Gender of antecedent: **Sagitta** (*arrow*) is feminine.
3. Number: *This (one)* and *that (one)* are both singular.
4. Selection: nominative feminine singular ⟶ **haec**
   nominative feminine singular ⟶ **illa**

Cupīdo duās sagittās habet. **Haec** est acūta; **illa** est obtūsa.
(sagittās: fem.; Haec: nom. fem. sing.; illa: nom. fem. sing.)

- *"****These*** *are my weapons," says Cupid. "I do not use* ***those****."*

1. Case: *These* = subject = nominative
   *those* = object = accusative
2. Gender of antecedent: **Arma** (*weapons*) is neuter.
3. Number: *These* and *those* are both plural.
4. Selection: nominative neuter plural ⟶ **haec**
   accusative neuter plural ⟶ **illa**

"**Haec** sunt mea arma," dīcit Cupīdo. "**Illa** nōn adhibeō."
(Haec: nom. neut. pl.; arma: neut.; Illa: acc. neut. pl.)

## What is a Relative Pronoun?

A **RELATIVE PRONOUN** is a word that introduces a subordinate clause. This kind of clause is called a **RELATIVE CLAUSE** because it *relates* or *refers back* to a word in another clause (the antecedent). The relative pronoun serves two purposes:

1. As a pronoun it stands for a noun or another pronoun previously mentioned called its **ANTECEDENT**.

    This is the woman ***who*** caused the war.

    antecedent (woman) — relative pronoun (***who***)

2. It introduces a **SUBORDINATE CLAUSE**, that is a group of words having a subject and verb separate from the main clause (see pp. 111, 114).

    main clause: This is the woman — subordinate clause: ***who*** caused the war.

    The above subordinate clause is also called a **RELATIVE CLAUSE** because it starts with a relative pronoun (*who*). The relative pronoun (*who*) connects the subordinate clause to its antecedent (*woman*).

In English and in Latin, the choice of the relative pronoun will depend on the function of the relative pronoun in the relative clause. You must train yourself to go through the following steps:

1. Find the relative clause.
2. Determine the function of the relative pronoun in the relative clause.
    - Is it the subject?
    - Is it the direct object?
    - Is it the indirect object?
    - Is it an object of a preposition?
    - Is it a possessive modifier?

3. Select the proper relative pronoun based on the antecedent.
   - Is it a person?
   - Is it a thing?

4. Select the proper form of the relative pronoun based on steps 1-3.

**In English:** Here are the English relative pronouns.

1. Subject of the relative clause:

   - ***who*** (if the antecedent is a person)

     This is the hero *who* won the war.
     (hero = antecedent)

     *Who* is the subject of *won.*

   - ***which*** (if the antecedent is a thing)

     This is the war *which* was fought at Troy.
     (war = antecedent)

     *Which* is the subject of *was fought.*

   - ***that*** (if the antecedent is a thing)

     This is the face *that* launched a thousand ships.
     (face = antecedent)

     *That* is the subject of *launched.*

2. Object of the verb in the relative clause: These pronouns are sometimes omitted in English. We have indicated them in parentheses. They must be expressed in Latin.

- ***whom*** (if the antecedent is a person)

This is the hero (*whom*) Hector killed.
antecedent (hero) — subject of relative clause (Hector)

*Whom* is the direct object of *killed.*

- ***which*** (if the antecedent is a thing)

This is the wooden horse (*which*) the Greeks built.
antecedent (horse) — subject of relative clause (Greeks)

*Which* is the direct object of *built.*

- ***that*** (if the antecedent is a thing)

Troy is the city (*that*) the Greeks destroyed.
antecedent (city) — subject of relative clause (Greeks)

*That* is the direct object of *destroyed.*

3. Possessive modifier

- ***whose*** (if the antecedent is a person)

Helen was the woman *whose* face launched a thousand ships.
antecedent (woman) — possessive modifying *face* (whose)

Only the relative pronoun for persons shows different case forms in English: *who* (subjective), *whom* (objective), and *whose* (possessive). The relative pronouns *which* and *that* do not change form for different cases.

The relative pronoun enables you to combine two short simple sentences into one complex sentence.

- Sentence A: That is the hero.
  Sentence B: He won the war.

You can combine Sentence A and Sentence B by replacing the subject pronoun *he* with the relative pronoun *who.*

That is the hero *who won the war.*

*Who won the war* is the relative clause. It does not express a complete thought, and it is introduced by a relative pronoun.

*Who* stands for the noun *hero. Hero* is called the antecedent of *who.* Notice that the antecedent stands immediately before the relative pronoun which introduces the clause giving additional information about the antecedent.

*Who* serves as the subject of the verb *won* in the relative clause.

- Sentence A: Hector was the son of Priam.
  Sentence B: Achilles slew him.

You can combine Sentence A and Sentence B by replacing the object pronoun *him* with the relative pronoun *whom.*

Hector, *whom Achilles slew,* was the son of Priam.

*Whom Achilles slew* is the relative clause.

*Whom* stands for the noun *Hector.* Hector is the antecedent. Notice again that the antecedent comes immediately before the relative pronoun.

*Whom* serves as the direct object of the relative clause. (*Achilles* is the subject.)

- Sentence A: Helen is a beautiful woman.
  Sentence B: Paris ran away with her.

You can combine Sentence A and Sentence B by replacing the preposition + personal pronoun (*with her*) with the preposition + relative pronoun (*with whom*).

Helen is the beautiful woman *with whom* Paris ran away.

In colloquial English, you could combine these two sentences by saying:

Helen is the beautiful woman Paris ran away with.

To say this in Latin, you would need to change the structure to avoid ending the sentence with a preposition. Take the preposition *with* from the end of the sentence (a preposition separated from its object is called a dangling preposition, see p. 193), and use it to begin the relative clause. Put it right at the place where you connect the two clauses. Then you need to add the relative pronoun *whom* right after the preposition *with*:

| | |
|---|---|
| Helen is the beautiful woman Paris ran away *with*. → | Helen is the beautiful woman *with whom* Paris ran away. |

Restructuring English sentences which contain a dangling preposition will help you to identify the relative clause and will give you the first step toward determining the correct English and Latin word order. It will also teach you the difference between the use of *who* and *whom* in English.

| | |
|---|---|
| Venus is the goddess Paris gave the golden apple *to*. → | Venus is the goddess *to whom* Paris gave the golden apple. |
| Priam is the king we are reading *about*. → | Priam is the king *about whom* we are reading. |

**In Latin:** There are case forms for relative pronouns in all five cases, depending on the function of the relative pronoun in the relative clause. The antecedent plays an important role in the selection of the relative pronoun. In Latin, it matters not only whether the antecedent is a person or a thing, but also whether the antecedent is masculine, feminine, or neuter by grammatical gender (see p. 7) and whether it is singular or plural. For example, if you have the word *island* as the antecedent of *which,* you must use the feminine singular relative pronoun since *island* is feminine in Latin.

*The* ***island, which*** *you see, is very beautiful.*

antecedent — relative pronoun

Gender of antecedent: **Īnsula** (*island*) is feminine.
Number of antecedent: *Island* is singular.

**Īnsula**, **quam** spectās, est pulcherrima.

ant. — rel. pr. acc. obj. of **spectās**

fem. sing.

Consult your textbook for the complete declension of the relative pronoun, in all cases, singular and plural.

N.B.: Although the relative pronouns *who, whom, which* and *that* are sometimes omitted in English, they must always be expressed in Latin.

**In English:** We can say either:

1. Is that the house *that* we visited?

   or

2. Is that the house we visited?

1. Is there anyone here *whom* you know?

   or

2. Is there anyone here you know?

**In Latin:** Since the relative pronoun can never be omitted, only Sentence 1 above contains all the necessary words to be expressed in Latin.

To find the correct relative pronoun in Latin you must go through the following steps:

1. Recognize the relative clause: restructure the English relative clause if there is a dangling preposition.[1]

2. Find the antecedent: to what word in the main clause does the relative clause refer?

3. Determine the gender and number of the antecedent.
   - Is it masculine, feminine or neuter?
   - Is it singular or plural?

4. Determine the function and therefore the case of the relative pronoun within the relative clause.
   - Is it the subject? ⟶ nominative
   - Is it the direct object? ⟶ accusative
   - Is it an indirect object? ⟶ dative
   - Is it the object of a preposition? ⟶ accusative or ablative
   - Is it a possessive modifier? ⟶ genitive

5. Select the proper form of the relative pronoun based on steps 1-4.

Let us apply the steps outlined above to the following sentences in order to select the correct relative pronoun:

- *The woman* ***who*** *caused the war was Helen.*

  1. Relative clause: *who caused the war*
  2. Antecedent: *woman*
  3. Number and gender of antecedent: **Fēmina** is feminine singular.
  4. Function of *who* within relative clause: subject = nominative
  5. Selection: nominative feminine singular ⟶ **quae**

  Fēmina **quae** causam bellī dedit erat Helena.

- *Is this the kingdom* ***(that)*** *the Greeks destroyed?*

  1. Relative clause: *(that) the Greeks destroyed*
     Remember that the relative pronoun must always be stated in Latin.
  2. Antecedent: *the kingdom*

[1]A preposition which is the last word in the sentence (see p. 193).

3. Number and gender of antecedent: **Regnum** is neuter singular.
4. Function of (*that*) within relative clause: direct object = accusative
5. Selection: accusative neuter singular ——• **quod**

Hocne est regnum **quod** Graecī vastāvērunt?

- *Circe, **whose** power was very great, kept Ulysses in her palace.*

1. Relative clause: *whose power was very great*
2. Antecedent: *Circe*
3. Number and gender of antecedent: **Circē** is feminine singular (name of a person).
4. Function of *whose* within relative clause: possessive modifier connecting Circe with her power = genitive
5. Selection: genitive feminine singular ——• **cuius**

Circē, **cuius** potentia erat maxima, Ulixem in rēgiā retinēbat.

- *Where is the woman you ran away with?*

| | |
|---|---|
| Where is the woman you ran away *with*? ——• | Where is the woman *with whom* you ran away? |

1. Relative clause: *with whom you ran away*
2. Antecedent: *woman*
3. Number and gender of antecedent: **Fēmina** is feminine singular.
4. Function of *whom* within relative clause: object of preposition *with*. **Cum** always takes an ablative object.
5. Selection: ablative feminine singular: ——• **quā**

Ubi est fēmina **quācum** confūgistī?

(**cum quā**) **cum** is frequently attached to its object.

- *The temples (**which**) we are visiting are very beautiful.*

1. Relative clause: *(which) we are visiting*
2. Antecedent: *temples*
3. Number and gender of antecedent: **Templa** is neuter plural.
4. Function of *which* within relative clause: direct object = accusative
5. Selection: accusative neuter plural ——• **quae**

Templa **quae** visitāmus sunt pulcherrima.

- *These are the swords you were talking about.*

| These are the swords you were talking *about.* → | These are the swords *about which* you were talking. |
|---|---|

1. Relative clause: *about which you were talking*
2. Antecedent: *swords*
3. Number and gender of antecedent: **Gladiī** is masculine plural.
4. Function of *which* within relative clause: object of preposition. **Dē** always takes the ablative case.
5. Selection: ablative masculine plural → **quibus**

Hī sunt gladiī **dē quibus** loquēbāris.

As a final rule, memorize this sentence: The relative pronoun takes its gender and number from its antecedent, but its case from its use in its own clause.

## What is a Preposition?

A **PREPOSITION** is a word which shows the relationship between a noun or pronoun and another word in the sentence. Prepositions may indicate position, direction, time, manner, means or agent. A preposition introduces an object in a **PREPOSITIONAL PHRASE.**

**In English:** Here are examples of prepositions:

- to show position

  Danae was imprisoned ***in*** a dungeon.
  Perseus was set adrift ***on*** water.

- to show direction

  Jupiter came ***to*** her in a shower of gold.
  The chest drifted ***toward*** an island.
  The order ***from*** the king was cruel.

- to show time

  Perseus lived ***for*** many years on the island.
  ***After*** several years the king wanted to marry Danae.

- to show manner

  Danae reacted ***with*** disgust.
  Perseus left ***in*** anger.

- to show means

  Perseus killed Medusa ***with*** a sword.
  He flew ***by*** means of winged sandals.

- to show agent

  Perseus was given winged sandals ***by*** the god Mercury.
  Medusa was killed ***by*** Perseus.

The noun or pronoun which the preposition connects to the rest of the sentence is called the OBJECT OF THE PREPOSITION. The preposition and its object together make up a **PREPOSITIONAL PHRASE.**

To help you recognize prepositional phrases, here is a story where the prepositional phrases are in italics and the preposition which introduces each phrase is in boldface.

> Because it was foretold that his grandson would kill him, the king ***of*** *Argos* imprisoned his daughter Danae ***in*** *a dungeon* so that she would not bear a child. Jupiter, the king ***of*** *the gods*, fell ***in*** *love* ***with*** *her* and came ***to*** *her* ***in*** *a shower* ***of*** *gold* ***in*** *her*

*prison.* She bore the hero Perseus, but both mother and child were set adrift ***in** a chest **on** water.* The chest drifted ***to** an island* where the two were rescued and taken ***to** the king.* That king fell ***in** love **with** Danae* and wanted to marry her. He sent Perseus to bring back the head ***of** Medusa,* when the hero, now grown, objected ***to** the marriage.* Anyone who looked ***at** Medusa* was turned ***to** stone.* Perseus cut off her head ***by** flying* backwards and *looking **at** her **in** his polished shield.* He then turned the king ***to** stone **on** his return.* Eventually he did kill his grandfather ***by** accident.*

**In Latin:** You will have to memorize prepositions as vocabulary items. In Latin all prepositions take objects in a particular case: accusative or ablative. When you learn a preposition, you must learn which case it requires for its object. Below are examples of prepositions which take objects in the accusative and/or in the ablative:

- an accusative object

  Arca **ad īnsulam** portāta est.
  
  acc. fem. sing.
  **Ad** always requires an accusative object.

  *The chest was carried **toward an island.***

- an ablative object

  Arca **ā piscatōre** inventa est.
  
  abl. masc. sing.
  **Ā (ab)** always requires an ablative object.

  *The chest was found **by a fisherman.***

The prepositions **in** (*in/on*) and **sub** (*under*) govern either the accusative when motion is indicated by the verb or the ablative when there is no motion.

*Danae remained* ***on the island.***
Danaē **in īnsulā** mānsit.

abl. fem. sing.
**In** governs the ablative since there is no motion in the verb.

*The chest was thrown* ***into the water.***
Arca **in aquam** iacta est.

acc. fem. sing.
**In** governs the accusative since there is motion in the verb.

In learning how to use Latin prepositions, there are several important rules to remember.

1. You must be careful to distinguish in English between prepositional phrases introduced by *to* indicating the indirect object (see p. 32) and *to* indicating direction toward a location.

- *to* indicating an indirect object

The action of the verb is done to or for someone or something. The prepositional phrase answers the question *TO WHAT* or *TO WHOM.*

*He gave a theater* ***to the city.***

The indirect object can be expressed either by *to* as above or by reversing the word order and putting the indirect object without the *to* before the direct object.

*He gave* ***the city*** *a theater.*

He gave the theater *to what?* To the city.
*The city* is the indirect object.

In Latin, the indirect object is expressed by using the dative case alone, without a preposition.

**Urbī** theātrum dōnāvit.

indirect object =
dative femine singular

- *to* indicating direction toward a location

The preposition *to* is used in a phrase of direction towards a location. It answers the question *TO WHERE.*

*He was walking **to the city.***

He was walking *to where?* To the city.
*The city* is the object of the preposition.

In Latin, the preposition **ad** (*to*) is followed by the location in the accusative case.

**Ad urbem** ambulābat.

object of preposition **ad** =
accusative feminine singular

2. Every language uses prepositions differently. Do not assume that the same preposition is used in Latin as in English, or that one is even used at all (see p. 36).

| English | | Latin |
|---|---|---|
| preposition used | → | no preposition |
| to look *at* | | spectāre + accusative |

The king ***looked at the head.***
Rēx **caput spectāvit.**

accusative

| | |
|---|---|
| to wait *for* | exspectāre + accusative |

*The children **are waiting for their mother.***
Līberī **mātrem exspectant.**

accusative

no preposition used ——• preposition may be used

to approach — appropinquāre + **ad** + accusative

*The chest* ***approached the island.***
Arca **ad īnsulam appropinquāvit.**
accusative

to enter — intrāre + **in** + accusative

***They entered the house.***
**In casam intrāvērunt.**
accusative

Also, many prepositions which must be used in English are unnecessary in Latin because of the case system. For example:

- *of* (possessive) = genitive (no preposition)

  *The mother* ***of the boy*** *is here.*
  Mater **puerī** adest.

- *with* (by means of) = ablative (no preposition)

  *Perseus killed Medusa* ***with a sword.***
  Perseus **gladiō** Medūsam necāvit.

- *on, at* (location) = locative (no preposition)

  *They lived* ***at home.***
  **Domī** habitābant.

These are just samples. Your Latin textbook treats this subject under the use of the various case forms.

3. The position of a preposition in an English sentence is much more variable than in a Latin sentence. Spoken English

sometimes places the preposition at the end of the sentence far from its object; this shift results in what is called a **DANGLING PREPOSITION**. Formal English places the preposition within the sentence or at the beginning of a question before its object. Look at the position of the preposition in the following sentences:

| Spoken English | Formal English |
|---|---|
| This is the man I spoke *with.* | This is the man *with whom* I spoke. |
| That is the city I'm going *to.* | That is the city *to which* I am going. |
| That is the hero I'm talking *about.* | That is the hero *about whom* I am talking. |

The position of a preposition in a Latin sentence is the same as in formal English; that is, it is never at the end of a sentence. Nearly all Latin prepositions precede their objects.

When expressing an English sentence in Latin, remember to restructure any dangling prepositions; when you do, you will be able to find the object of the preposition and put it in its proper case in both English and Latin.

Look at the English sentences when they are translated into Latin:

- *Here is the man I spoke* ***with.***

| |
|---|
| Here is the man I spoke *with.*—► Here is the man *with whom* I spoke. |

Hic est vir **cum quō** locūtus sum.

object of preposition **cum** = ablative

- *That is the city I'm going* ***to.***

| |
|---|
| That is the city I'm going *to.*—► That is the city *to which* I am going. |

Illa est urbs **ad quam** eō.

object of preposition **ad** = accusative

- *That is the hero I'm talking* ***about.***

| |
|---|
| That is the hero I'm talking *about.* → That is the hero *about whom* I am talking. |

Ille est hērōs **dē quō** dīcō.

object of preposition **dē** = ablative

## What is an Interjection?

An INTERJECTION is a cry, an expression of strong feeling or emotion. It is *thrown into* (from the Latin **interjectum**) the sentence, usually at the beginning, and stands apart from the grammar of the sentence.

**In English:** There are a great variety of such emotional words, including most words of swearing and profanity. They belong to both written and spoken language, but more often to the latter. An interjection is separated from the main clause by a comma and the sentence usually ends with an exclamation mark.

*Ah,* how beautiful she is!
*Alas,* wretched me!

**In Latin:** A similar variety of emotional words exists in Latin and includes the equivalents of expressions of awe, anger, and the evoking of a deity. An interjection is invariable; i.e. it never changes form. It usually introduces a sentence which ends with an exclamation mark.

***Ā***, quam pulchra est!
***Ah,*** *how beautiful she is!*

**Heu**, mē miserum!
***Alas,*** *wretched me!*

**Mehercule**, illud nōn sinam!
***By Hercules,*** *I will not allow that!*

# Index